Eating and Drinking at the Welcome Table

To Patrick —

Bill Mc Elvaney —

I deeply appreciate the ecumenical ministry which you lead & share!

Eating and Drinking at the Welcome Table

THE HOLY SUPPER FOR ALL PEOPLE

William K. McElvaney

Chalice Press
St. Louis, Missouri

All scripture quotations, unless otherwise indicated, are from the *New Revised Standard Version Bible*, copyright 1989, Division of Christian Education of the National Council of the Churches of Christ in the USA. Used by permission.

Cover design: Arista Graphics

Art direction: Elizabeth Wright

Interior design: Elizabeth Wright

This book is printed on acid-free, recycled paper.

Visit Chalice Press on the World Wide Web at
www.chalicepress.com

10 9 8 7 6 5 4 3 2 1   98 99 00 01 02 03

Library of Congress Cataloging-in-Publication Data

McElvaney, William K., 1928–
    Eating and drinking at the welcome table: the Holy Supper for all people / by William K. McElvaney.
        p.   cm.
    Includes bibliographical references.
    ISBN 0-8272-0812-X
    1. Lord's Supper. I. Title.
    BV825.2.M43   1998   98-31360
    264'.36—dc21   CIP

Printed in the United States of America

For my friend William M. Finnin, Jr.,
in appreciation for many shared celebrations
of the eucharist and many conversations
about things that matter.

The author's proceeds from the sale of
Eating and Drinking at the Welcome Table
will support The Greater Dallas Community of Churches,
The Dallas Peace Center, and *Proyecto Adelante*
(a provider of legal services to refugees).

I'm gonna eat at the welcome table, Allelu.
I'm gonna eat and drink with my Jesus, Allelu.
I'm gonna join with sisters, brothers, Allelu.
Here all the world will find a welcome, Allelu.
We're gonna feast on milk and honey, Allelu.

from "I'm Gonna Eat at the Welcome Table"
African American spiritual
(see *Chalice Hymnal* 424)

Contents

Acknowledgments

Meister Eckhart, the 13th–14th century mystic, once said that there is finally only one prayer. It consists of two words: "Thank you."

Eating and Drinking at the Welcome Table has been nurtured by more thank you's than I can recall. My own growing appreciation for the eucharist over the years owes its first thank you to the God revealed for centuries to our Jewish brothers and sisters in what Christians refer to as sacramental ways, including bread and wine...and revealed to those of us who call ourselves Christians in the bread and wine of Jesus Christ in the upper room and on the road to Emmaus. Subsequently, thank you goes to the long line of faithful Jews who provided and projected a sacramental understanding of life, and to the long line of faithful Christians who have preserved the sacred story in the form of an embodied Word.

The content of the book, especially chapter 2, will provide specific ways and settings in which my own eucharistic journey has developed and the specific thank you's appropriate. Suffice it here to express indebtedness to the writings of James F. White, especially for the justice implications of the sacraments. I have learned much from Marjorie Procter-Smith, a faculty colleague at Perkins School of Theology, Southern Methodist University.

During my fifteen years as pastor of United Methodist congregations, rural and suburban, many laypersons provided affirmation, encouragement, and reflection on eucharistic understanding and practice. In addition most of the material herein has been explored with give and take in a variety of ecumenical settings involving both laity and clergy from Protestant and Roman Catholic traditions. These include seminary classes, pastors' conferences, local churches, and chaplains' retreats. Thank you for insights and perspectives from many points of view!

I extend special gratitude to Will Finnin, Chaplain of Southern Methodist University, with whom I shared four years of regular celebration of word and table at Southern Methodist University Worship. Many of the suggestions of four insightful readers have been included in the completed work. I owe many thank you's to Walter Brueggemann, Paul Escamilla, Jane Marshall, and Marjorie Procter-Smith for gifts of time and wisdom.

The title of this book is taken from the words of an African American spiritual titled "I'm Gonna Eat at the Welcome Table" (see separate page). Thank you to those who made this spiritual possible. What rich and empowering images!

Once again I owe a huge thanks to Ann I. Ralston for unfailing graciousness and competence in preparing and repairing the manuscript several times over. Ann, you get the first copy!

Preface

I have a passionate conviction that the sacrament of the Lord's table can become an informing and transforming experience for Christians of every tradition. Worshipers whom I have talked to and communed with come from at least two places in regard to the eucharist.

Some of you reading these words most likely experience the Lord's Supper as a routine ritual, an exercise that must have some meaning to *other* worshipers. Through the years many committed Christians have said to me, "I just don't get it when it comes to participating in the body and blood thing. I must not be a sacramental type." Other readers bring a favorable impression of the Lord's table or altar, perhaps even a profound appreciation, yet with an eager willingness to consider deeper and wider implications.

During something like the past fifteen years of my forty years of ordained ministry I have developed a great love for the eucharist. Better said, the eucharist has embraced me at a much deeper level than I could have possibly foreseen. I had always been one who emphasized preaching as the center of the church's worship. Now I advocate word and table as the center, a direction now recognized by many Protestant hymnals and books of worship. As I have taught, planned, and celebrated liturgy, I have become aware that sacramentality in mutual relationship with sermon mentality is not what some refer to as "high" church but rather early or apostolic church and the most normative church at worship through the ages.

For me the eucharist has become an epicenter of understanding and experiencing the meaning and implications of the Christian gospel. In the pages and chapters that follow my purpose and intent look like this:

- to invite you to rethink the place of the Lord's Supper in your life and in the practice of your worshiping community;

- to encourage you to recall and reflect on your earliest and most recent memories of the eucharist and to allow me to share my own eucharistic journey;

- to foster a growing awareness of the eucharist as both profoundly personal and vigorously prophetic;

- to reflect on some implications for the church living the eucharist in today's world;

- to raise some issues regarding eucharistic liturgies, logistics, and language; and

- to coax hearts and minds towards the eucharist as the basic picture and portrayal of what it means to live the gospel faithfully and joyfully.

Eating and Drinking at the Welcome Table is written for an ecumenical readership, both laity and clergy, although mainly from a Protestant perspective. I have in mind adult classes and other study groups in local churches and retreats. I'm grateful for my own journey of discovery over the years as a pastor, seminary administrator, and faculty member. So I am bold to believe that clergy, too, can benefit personally and in your calling from some stretching for fresh visions of the eucharist.

I have combined biblical, theological, and experiential components for our road not always traveled into the eucharist. This book is *not* a historical treatise as such, although historical components will appear as appropriate to the subject at hand. This book is a testament of devotion to the eucharist, concerned primarily with discernment and discovery through reflection and experience. See the works cited for readings that include excellent historical analyses of the eucharist.

Our experiences of holy communion and the interpretations we render cannot be separated from the age in which we live, the particular contours of our era, and the neighbors whom God sets before us. As far back as 1965, before the eucharist came to be central to my faith, I wrote an article for the *Christian Advocate* entitled, "Is Our Communion Liturgy Christian?" The concern raised was the near absence of references to our neighbor in the liturgy then in use. We consider a sacrament for all time and yet for our specific time at the intersection of the twentieth and twenty-first centuries and beyond. When we eat and drink at the welcome table, pertinent questions call our names and demand to be heard. The lesions of humanity are legion and are forever connected by this sacrament with origins of liberation. What does it mean to offer and receive the body of Christ when multitudes of our neighbors in the world are starving? Or the blood of Christ poured for you and me when so much blood is shed daily on our streets of violence? What are the implications of visually and viscerally remembering the Prince of Peace in a nuclear age? What kind of difference might it make to receive the Lord's supper, a meal related to the Passover tradition, in view of the Holocaust and the long history of anti-Semitic elements in Christian theology and practice? In a world unsafe for women, and all too often in the church as well, does the eucharist make a difference?

What can it mean that we ingest the bread and wine at the table or altar next to one who just this week was presented a diagnosis of multiple myeloma? Or experienced the loss of a child? Or the loss of a job due to corporate downsizing? Obviously these are huge and difficult questions, but we dare not extend our hearts and hands to receive the bread and wine of Jesus Christ as though the church existed solely for the benefit of its own members. These questions will meet us again on the journey ahead, as well as others like them.

A Word about Words

Some Protestant church traditions use the terms "the Lord's supper," "holy communion," or just plain "communion." Other church bodies are more likely to be familiar with the term "eucharist." Still others are at home with several of these words. Likewise some are most likely to speak of the Lord's table while others speak of the altar. Altar-table is also heard.

This book will use all of these terms. There can be distinctions in the meanings of these terms, some of which will be explained. The premise of this book, however, is that the rich and diverse meanings, of the sacrament (some say "ordinance") embrace all of these terms. The particularity of words is of course important, but words should not obscure the underlying commonality of Christian experiences of bread and chalice rooted in Jesus Christ. An ecumenical spirit beckons us to be user-friendly with an array of terms relating to the table sacrament.

Two Caveats

Throughout the book reference will be made to word and table as basic components of Christian worship, with special emphasis on the Lord's supper or eucharist. It is well to remember, however, that sermon and sacrament are part of the larger liturgical setting. Preserving and proclaiming the sacred story is also accomplished through song, scripture, silence, prayers, gestures, visual arts, and other means. The interaction of God and people is a multi-layered experience drawing on a rich history of liturgical treasures. Some services, such as morning and evening prayer, depend primarily on scripture and prayer and include neither sermon nor sacrament.

Secondly, I have great respect for the classical worship of Quakers, who depend on neither sermon nor sacrament as they are known in many church traditions. Without either sermonic word or table, Quakers historically have been at the forefront of Christian social witness, far beyond the strength of their numbers. Thus, when I write with passion regarding the benefits of sacrament taken in faith, my purpose is neither to disparage the worship of other Christian practices nor to limit the means of grace by which God is revealed.

We're ready now to move on. I hope my readers will bring an inquiring mind, a heart of hope, and whatever eucharistic language with which they are familiar: the Lord's supper, the eucharist, holy communion; or other names: table, altar, altar-table. The deepest meanings of the sacrament, thank God, transcend denominational labels and our most sophisticated attempts to own the mystery of grace.

1

If You Had to Choose: Sermon or Sacrament?

For the bread which you have broken,
for the wine which you have poured,
for the words which you have spoken,
now we give you thanks, O Lord.
Louis F. Benson, 1924
(*Chalice Hymnal* 411)

I invite you in this first chapter to consider a fiendish question and to make an outlandish imaginary choice. Try this: If you had to choose between the sermon and the sacrament of holy communion for the rest of your life, which would you choose and why? If you choose preaching, you will never again receive communion. If you choose the eucharist, you will never hear another sermon as long as you live.

You may assume that you could choose the eucharistic liturgy of your preference and that scripture would be part of the service. Likewise, if you were to choose preaching, there would be appropriate scripture. Remember, you are choosing for yourself. Would your choice be different if you were choosing for the church instead of for yourself? This exercise is merely a teaching tool for clarifying our hidden preferences and priorities. As I will attempt to demonstrate later in the chapter, word and table, sermon and sacrament have belonged together in the early church and in much of church history. *My ultimate aim* is to encourage the unity of the spoken word and the visible word, to suggest how they are mutually supportive, and to remind us of the need for diverse ways of hearing, receiving, and participating in God's self-giving.

Now back to our imaginary choice. I began trying this question on various groups in 1985, including lay groups, pastors' conferences, seminary students, and chaplains (hospital, prison, military, and industrial). Before responding to the question of choice between sermon and communion, those groups would study at least a historical overview of word and table. Our study included liturgical updating since the 1962-65 Vatican II Conference, which strongly impacted both Roman Catholic and Protestant recovery of word and table.

In presenting the question over the last twelve years to various groups I have suggested that limits, even imaginary ones as in this case, help us to focus on what seems most essential and why. If circumstances permit, I insist that each person think about it overnight or until our next session. When we come together again, we have a show of hands, revealing our choices, and begin sharing the reasons for our position. "Talk to each other," I usually say. An invigorating theological and liturgical discussion *always* follows. The procedure puts people in touch with thoughts and feelings about both sermon and sacrament and has the benefit of hearing why others in the group have chosen similarly or otherwise. It's a good sign when most participants indicate that it was a difficult choice, or that they will be more open to the choice not made due to the convincing experience shared by others.

Presently in this chapter, after you have had the opportunity to reflect on the choice individually or with a group,

I will put forth the composite results of what dozens of groups have said and the reasons given. Perhaps you have already responded in your mind with a preference for either sermon or sacrament. Or perhaps not. See if the following brief excursion into some snapshots of sermon and sacrament history alters your consideration or makes it more difficult.

Word and Table in History: Some Contours

During the two thousand years of Christian history, word and table have been held together more often than any other pattern of worship. Thus far in this first chapter we have recognized the importance of our own experience and preferences. Whatever our personal history of the Lord's supper and preaching may be, our accumulated experience represents where we are at the present time. I could have begun this chapter with some historical background to word and table, but I wanted you to name your own experience first. No recounting of church tradition—actually, traditions—can or should lead us to deny our own experiences. Yet as Christians we are ill-advised to measure our faith and witness solely on personal experience.

United Methodists sometimes utilize a fourfold framework from which to shape understanding and practice of the faith: scripture, tradition, reason, and experience. Derived from the ministry of John Wesley, this so-called quadrilateral often serves as a testing ground for directions and decisions. I expect that many denominations utilize something like this combination in responding to issues of authority, that is, "Who says so and on what basis?"

Some brief contours of scripture and traditions will assist us in being more fully aware of our multiple heritage. The study of liturgical development over the centuries can be immensely rewarding intellectually and spiritually. There is much to learn from our faith forebears about word and table, and some things *not* to emulate. Following are a few biblical and historical developments which can inform our understanding. My hope for this section is twofold. One is that it will be pertinent to the immediate concern of this chapter. Another is that it will stimulate your further hunger and thirst for inquiry into this field of study.

The New Testament provides two central sources for the worship of the first Christians. It also informs us that these two sources quickly came together providing a basic pattern, with variables, for the first fifteen centuries of Christian worship. From the Jewish temple and synagogue tradition came scripture, psalms, prayer, and spoken word or sermon. These became solidified as the initial part of Christian worship services, what we sometimes refer to as "the service of the word." From the upper room came the sacred meal, or visible Word, with roots in the Jewish Passover tradition and Jesus' table fellowship with disciples, women, tax collectors, sinners, the self-righteous, and hungry crowds. The full meal became a representative meal of bread and wine, later named a sacrament, and followed the spoken word as the second major act of Christian worship, what is often called "the service of the table."

We read of the first Christians attending the temple and breaking bread in their homes (Acts 2:46). In or near the village of Emmaus we are told how Jesus interpreted scripture and broke bread at table with his followers, an account of spoken word and table hosted by the risen Christ (Luke 24:28-35). Again and again spoken word and visible word are lifted up as basic to Christian worship. In Luke 4 we hear Jesus' preaching in the synagogue at Nazareth. In 1 Corinthians 11 we have apparently the earliest New Testament telling of the table tradition and Jesus' words of invitation. As Paul says to the Corinthian Christians, "I received from the Lord what I also handed on to you" (1 Corinthians 11:23-26). To Paul, receiving from the apostolic tradition was tantamount to receiving from the Lord.

At this point we are not exploring the meaning of the table communion as much as noting its early presence along with the spoken word. Succeeding chapters will lift up various interpretations of this configuration. For now it is worth recognizing that word and table together preceded the New Testament itself, the formation of creed and doctrine, and all but the most rudimentary form's of church organization. From the earliest Christian beginnings came the normative worship combining sermon mentality and sacramentality. One of our earliest records of Christian worship comes from the writing of Justin Martyr in his First Apology, written in Rome approximately 155 A.D. Here is a second-century excerpt:

Second Century	Today's Equivalent
And on the day called Sunday an *assembly* is held in one place of all who	*Gathering/Entrance*
live in town or country, and the *records* of the apostles or .writings of the prophets are read for as long as time allows.	*Scripture*
Then, when the reader has finished, the president in a *discourse* admonishes and exhorts us to imitate these good things.	*Sermon/Word proclaimed*
Then we all *stand up together and offer prayers;* and as we said before, when we have	*Prayers of the People/ Responses*
finished praying, *bread and wine* and water are brought up, and the president likewise	*Presentation of Gifts*
offers prayers and thanksgivings to the best of his ability, and the people assent, saying	*Great Thanksgiving*
the Amen; and there is a *distribution*, and everyone participates in (the elements) over which thanks have been given; and they are sent through the deacons to those who are not present.	*Communion*
And the wealthy who so desire give *what they wish*, as each chooses; and what is collected is deposited with the president.	*Offering*
He helps orphans and widows, and those who through sickness or any other cause are in need, and those in prison, and strangers sojourning among us; in a word, he takes *care of all those who are in need.*	*Outreach*

(Richardson 1953, 287)

This early pattern of congregational worship fusing word and table became virtually inseparable until the sixteenth century, except on rare special occasions. However, two cave-ats are necessary lest the impression be given that sermon and eucharist co-existed in somewhat equal prominence until the Protestant Reformation. During the Middle Ages the sermon became very secondary to the sacramental system. Excep-tions were the emphasis on preaching by the mendicant or-ders, such as Franciscans and Dominicans, and in the crusades, and some universities.

The other caution concerning fusion of word and table is that for almost a thousand years during the regular celebra-tion of mass, the laity seldom received communion more than once a year, and even then, the bread or wafer only. Protes-tants usually assume that the Lord's supper, holy commun-ion, or the eucharist is equated with participation in bread and cup by the laity.

The sixteenth-century Protestant Reformation resulted, often unintentionally, in unbalancing sermon and sacrament in the opposite direction. Preaching became primary and the Lord's supper secondary, as James F. White explains:

> One cannot overestimate the ecstasy and joy that read-ing the scriptures in the vernacular and preaching the Word of God brought to many sixteenth-century Chris-tians as a new and unfamiliar form of communion with God. Such communion was so personal, so intimate, that it often simply made the visible word of the sacra-ments seem redundant and remote. That was not the intention but frequently the effect of the reformers' work. (White, *Protestant Worship* 1989, 14)

Thus, the reformers sought to challenge and correct the premises and abuses of the existing sacramental sys-tem, desiring to restore more frequent communion by the people on a faith basis, in the language of the people. Re-flecting on Luther's 1520 treatise on the sacramental sys-tem, "The Babylonian Captivity of the Church," White states:

This treatise represents a genuine paradigm shift, for it completely undercuts the ground on which the whole medieval sacramental system stood...

The final consequence was to move the central focus of Christian worship for Protestants from worship—which for lay people, had been almost entirely the sacrament—to one in which the sacraments became occasional intruders on a normal pattern of worship. No greater shift has ever occurred in Christian worship, either in East or West. (White, 1989, 36–37)

A long-range result of the Protestant Reformation was the triumph of the word-oriented synagogue tradition over the table tradition of the upper room. Despite John Wesley's practice and plea for regular eucharist, the fate of the Lutheran and Reformed movements befell the Methodists in America, and to some degree the Anglican/Episcopalian tradition. Among non-Catholics only the Christian Church (Disciples of Christ) and the Churches of Christ, both of North American origin, insisted on weekly observances of the Lord's supper.

However, times are changing. What I have called sermon mentality and sacramentality are in a process of restoration in relation to one another. Since the Second Vatican Council in the early 1960s Roman Catholics have given more attention to the homily or sermon, and Protestants have evidenced a stronger commitment to the eucharist. The result is a recovery and restoration of word and table as practiced in the early church. Seminary training and the development of liturgical resources by denominations have been part of this movement.

Making Sense out of Sermon and Sacrament Together

The previous historical sketch describes the normative nature of word and table together during the first fifteen centuries of the church, its continuation in some traditions, and its recovery on a wider basis in recent years. Yet a fair question remains: Are we bound to worship today in the way of the past? After all, we select from tradition that which we choose to continue and reject those parts that we are convinced need changing. Most of today's theological debates among and within denominations center on the question, By what authority do we retain or reject a certain concept or practice?

I believe there are sound and profound reasons for word and table together in our worship services besides merely repeating much of our past. Some of these reasons surely reflect the insights of Christians through the ages. Consider now certain aspects of that mutual reinforcement of word and table.

God's Ways of Giving

Sermon and sacrament together represent a fullness of God's grace, or as James White puts it, God's self-giving. Profound relationships involve both spoken word and touch in whatever ways physically possible. We should not be surprised that the New Testament healing stories always include either spoken word or some form of touch, and frequently both. Jesus speaks words of hope, encouragement, and challenge: "Take heart, daughter; your faith has made you well" (Matthew 9:22); "Come out of the man, you unclean spirit!" (Mark 5:8); "Do you want to be made well?" (John 5:6).

God also uses touch for healing and restoration. Jesus takes the little girl by the hand (Matthew 9:25). He touches the eyes of the blind men (Matthew 9:29). The woman with the hemorrhage touches the hem of his garment (Matthew 9:20). Always word or touch. Sometimes both.

So it does not surprise us that God uses both word and touch in the liturgy of the church. As we have already seen, spoken word in the form of calls to worship, scripture, prayers, and sermon represent words of God's grace for us and our responses to God, all with roots in the Jewish synagogue. Touch takes place in hugs and handshakes, passing the peace, which may combine touch and word, in settings of healing and anointing, and sacramentally in baptism and communion. The baby is touched or held by the representative (clergy) of the community. Water is touched in baptism, whether sprinkling, pouring, or immersion. We touch bread and chalice in whatever form. The Word is embodied in visible ways.

Can we even imagine a church without spoken word and touch? No one would speak and no one would touch. Boring! We would just look at each other like disembodied souls. Cold!

These multiple "idioms" of worship are carried out in life as the work of the people. Thus the spoken word of God and the interactive touch of God and people in worship become the way we go about ministry in the world. We seek to comfort a friend who's lost a loved one. Or we make a visit to the hospital. We're going to speak words of hope and encouragement—words of grace, we could say. Then we hold our friend's hand or offer a consoling embrace. "Take care," we say. "I'll be in touch," we add. Word and touch. We need both to receive and offer God's love and to love others.

It should not surprise us that the gifts of God are often misused. We have hurt others and have been hurt by words. Inappropriate touch is widespread in terms of harassment and exploitation, mostly of women and children. But that should not deter us from receiving the gifts of ministry and using them wisely.

Theologian Paul Tillich used to say that we could not be persons unless someone spoke to us and someone touched us. In a sense we could say that God has spoken to us and touched us in our gathering. Word and touch are indispensable for human identity and maturation as well as for faith formation. Why not celebrate, then, spoken word and embodied word every Lord's Day, thus recovering the fullness of both synagogue and the sacramental tradition from Jesus' many shared meals, including the upper room and the Emmaus experience?

Our Ways of Receiving

We learn in faith by both the cerebral and the sensory. Some of us respond most readily by listening. For these the sermon interprets scripture and offers a fresh word of hope and challenge. Others resonate with a broader use of sensory experience involving sight, touch, taste, and smell. For these persons the eucharist provides opportunity to embody firsthand the words of the sermon, the two together more faithfully involving the whole person. When you are able to share the "if you had to choose" question in a group, I'll guarantee that this paragraph's suggestions of diverse ways of receiving the Christian message will come alive in very specific ways.

Worship's Ways of Reaching Us

There is another dimension to our way of receiving. The plain unvarnished truth is that word and table rather than word without table makes for greater *assurance* of a viable message on a given Sunday. Plainly stated, there are inevitable Sundays when preaching is flat, uninspiring, and unedifying. In one way or another both laity and clergy know this. Even the very best preacher misses the mark from time to time. And even the most dedicated layperson is just "not with it" on some Sundays, even when the preaching is true and lively for the very next person in the pew. There can be *many* reasons for both situations, and there's no need to suggest them here.

I'm not implying that the Lord's supper is a divine guarantee of life-changing power on a given Lord's Day. Sometimes we just go through the motions, or, for some reason beyond our grasp, we are filled with all manner of doubt. Any act of worship can be a big fat zero at times. But just maybe the eucharist from time to time becomes a live alternative to a near-death sermon. It happens to me from time to time. Does it for you? When it does happen, give thanks to God.

Sermon and Sacrament Similarities

Although I have been suggesting the seeming differences between sermon and sacrament, the two are more alike than we sometimes realize. Recognizing how this is so can further enrich our worship experience.

Consider the sacramental in the sermon. The notion of the sacramental in biblical theology means that God is revealed to the eyes and ears of faith through earthen vessels, such as burning bushes, a rainbow, pillars of fire, a stone at Bethel, and bread and wine. In other words, certain objects are experienced in a way that discloses a divine presence. For Christians the primary and enduring sacramental reality is the revelation of God in and through Jesus Christ, the Word become flesh.

Maybe you have heard a preacher introduced like this prior to the sermon: "Brother (or Sister) Smith is going to 'break the bread of life' to us." There is a sacramental quality to the preaching of the Word through the medium of the preacher who in a sense may embody the word of God in voice and action.

Any preacher who has sensed herself or himself as a vehicle for the word of God knows the sacramental dimension of preaching. Sometimes it is clear to sermon listeners that God has come alive through the embodiment of the preacher's voice and persona.

Consider now the sermon or proclamation in the sacrament: "As often as you eat this bread and drink the cup, you *proclaim* the Lord's death until he comes." These words of Paul from 1 Corinthians 11:26 bring together the closeness of sermon and sacrament. The Greek word translated "proclaim" (from *katangello*) is the same Paul uses for preaching or proclamation elsewhere. For example, in Acts 15:36 Paul says to Barnabas, "Come, let us return and visit the believers in every city where we *proclaimed* the word of the Lord and see how they are doing." In 1 Corinthians 9:14 Paul, addressing the church concerning the rights of an apostle, declares,

"In the same way, the Lord commanded that those who proclaim the gospel should get their living by the gospel." So the sacrament preaches Christ in its own visible, embodied manner.

Testing Your Choice in a Group

Your task now, if possible, is to wrestle with and discuss "the choice" and your answers within a group. This could take place with a church school class, on a retreat, or, an informal gathering of friends. Share your experience and listen to those of others in the group. Probe the theological assumptions, the personal faith histories, and the revealed liturgical mentality. Don't forget, this is not finally about choosing up sides and defending positions with a bristly defense. It's intended to open minds and hearts to the remarkable resources that God has given the church for healing and transformation.

If You Had to Choose: Profiles of Many Voices

Now you can compare your response or the preferences of your group with the replies I have observed over a twelve-year period in various bodies. While the majority of participants have been United Methodists, the survey has included ecumenical groups with Presbyterians, Disciples, Lutherans, Episcopalians, Southern Baptists, and United Church of Christ members. Once again my purpose has been to initiate serious reflection on sermon and sacrament with the hope of unifying the two.

The first group to be tested with this outlandish question was a group of twenty-four laypersons attending a 1985 consultation at Saint Paul School of Theology in Kansas City, Missouri, where I was serving at the time. As indicated earlier, we shared some study in the history of worship in the Western church and recent developments. For several years the Lord's supper had become increasingly important to me. As a result, I was curious about the place of the sacrament in the minds and hearts of United Methodist laity, knowing that we were essentially a pulpit-centered church. Would there be a few of these midwestern "Word-fed" daughters and sons of John and Charles Wesley who would choose eucharist? I wondered. I asked them to think about it overnight and be prepared the next day to reveal their thoughts to each other. Upon returning home that evening, I decided to try this on my wife, Fran. She thought about it and replied, "That depends on who is doing the preaching!"

The next morning at the seminary we had a show of hands. I was shocked. Twelve and twelve. Frankly I had anticipated three or four out of twenty-four to select the eucharist. Was it not true in the experience of most United Methodist pastors over the years that worship attendance diminished on communion Sunday, usually the first Sunday of the month? What's going on here?

The reasons for choosing preaching went like this: Sermons interpret scripture year-round and relate biblical texts to everyday life; preaching can be educational, inspiring, and challenging; preaching called us into the faith, and without the spoken word we wouldn't know the meaning of the sacrament; preaching is our basic vehicle of evangelism; preaching has variety of content and offers insights from the Hebrew Bible as well as the New Testament.

Preferences for the eucharist sounded like the following: The sacrament is a direct experience of the living Christ through partaking the bread and cup; the eucharist is more dependable than preaching and does not have to rely on the speaking and interpretive skills of the preacher; the Lord's supper is more of a community experience than preaching, yet very personal and intimate; the communion calls forth a wider array of embodied experiences than just listening; children can more likely be participants in communion than in preaching (this depends on denominational practice).

Most of the twenty-four persons wrestling with these issues found the choice to be difficult. They indicated that hearing from brothers and sisters who made the opposite choice from their own was a worthwhile endeavor, opening new considerations. "Informative" and "enlightening" were terms used to describe the exercise. We concluded by giving thanks for both sermon and sacrament.

I have repeated this exercise many times over the past twelve years. Almost without exception the eucharist has prevailed in people's choices, whether clergy or laity and regardless of gender. I would expect Roman Catholics and members of the Christian Church (Disciples of Christ) to favor the sacramental act. After all, the mass constitutes the center of Roman Catholic worship, and for Disciples, the Christ who presides at the Lord's table is central.

What amazes me is the consistent choice of the Lord's supper over preaching by group after group of United Methodists, as well as by a much more limited numerical sampling of Presbyterians. I recall one United Methodist who said, "I've never heard a sermon that means as much as the Lord's supper." I replied, "Yes, but we can be thankful we don't actually have to make this excruciating choice between sermon and sacrament." To which he replied, "The United Methodist Church made this choice a long time ago. It decided the sermon was four times as important as the Lord's supper." He's right on, even if the church isn't.

I'll be the first to acknowledge that even twelve years of posing this choice to various groups represents a small percentage of worshipers. Even so, what might we learn from what has been accumulated? Here are some tentative observations.

1. Preaching has had a rather negligible value to many of these respondents, at least on a conscious level. After the first few years of hearing people's responses I began to wish that more people would choose preaching! It became clear to me that some of the lay respondents were trying to say in a nice way, "The preachers don't foul up the sacrament like they can the sermon. The eucharist we can count on!" This is hardly a plea to reduce preaching to once a month as a number of church bodies have done with the Lord's supper. But

it does suggest the need for much improvement in our preaching and perhaps a clear vision between preachers and congregations as to what is true and lively preaching.

2. There appears to be a greater appreciation for the eucharist than we generally recognize, at least in the United Methodist Church. Might it be true in other traditions? In recent years it has been clear that eucharist is being observed more frequently than on a monthly basis. A long-standing ethos of occasional communion is not changed overnight, but there are increasing numbers of congregations now celebrating weekly eucharist at one service or another.

3. One of the fascinating issues arising from the various groups has been that of age. Quite a few persons have said that early in their faith journey they unquestionably would have chosen preaching. It named the truth as we have come to see it and called us to faithfulness, they say. Now that they are in their fifth or sixth decade, they would choose the sacrament. It is as though they are saying, "Preaching has served an important function in our faith development and remains so. But the eucharist sustains us as we move into the latter stages of life. The sacrament has a timeless quality. The bread and cup make Christ come alive in a way not as dependent on human skills."

One person who chose eucharist put it this way: "I extrapolated backwards from an imaginary terminal illness. I realized if I were dying, I would not need another sermon. Just the bread and cup in my hands or on my lips if conditions permitted. Then I realized, if in death, why not in life?"

4. If these discussions in many groups over the past twelve years are any criterion, people's opinions of sermon and sacrament, born out of experience, can be altered and even transformed. While I have not been able to do a follow-up survey, it has seemed evident from the responses that many people are willing to hear fresh understandings of what sermons and sacraments can mean to their lives. New

appreciation comes from deeper and broader interpretations, especially of sacraments, from listening to the testimonies of others. Note that this process is laity learning from laity. Call it inspiration. Call it education. Call it fresh paradigms. The future is not bound by the past.

A stronger sacramental observance need not detract from preaching either emphasis-wise or time-wise. As I have tried to show, the two reinforce each other. Sermon and sacrament together offer the gifts of God in unified yet diverse manner. Together they offer verbal, visual, and visceral ways of interacting with God's presence. Together they provide the sound and shape of the church's mission to the world in the name of God.

2

Our Journeys with the Eucharist

What do I remember from my growing-up days about the Lord's supper? Several things. It was kind of scary and quite mysterious. But there was also something that drew me to it, although I couldn't describe what it was.
One worshiper's childhood memory

Can you recall any of your earliest memories of the Lord's supper? Are there one or more times through the years you can remember a special experience of the eucharist? For years I have invited adult classes and various individuals to share their remembrances of the sacrament while growing up or since confirmation. Many of these stories are so distinct and memorable that I can retrieve them virtually verbatim years later.

The telling of these stories gives voice to the history and wisdom of the faith community. A kaleidoscope of personal meanings and feelings, positive and negative, are laid bare for reflection and discovery. Naming a few special memories of the past can nurture the future. Hearing the treasured experiences of others can fortify our own faith.

Shared Eucharistic Experiences

This is the body of Jesus Christ broken for you. This is the blood of Christ shed for you. These words troubled me as a child, and I guess I've never gotten over it. I was frightened by the idea of drinking someone's blood. Later I thought of it as cannibalistic. It seemed spooky and gory. Maybe I was too much of a rationalist. It just didn't make sense to me.

I grew up in a church that did not serve communion to children until we were of age to be confirmed. When the Lord's supper or eucharist was celebrated, I went with my family to the front where my family received the elements, and I received a blessing. My parents did their best to explain the meaning of the sacrament. I didn't comprehend it at the time, but in some way I sensed what my parents were saying. I sensed that in a way beyond my understanding something terribly important had been done for me that I could not do for myself.

As a child I was allowed to receive the bread and the cup along with my family. This was more fun than the sermon for me, and besides that, the communion gave me a sense of belonging, just like eating at our table at home.

We weren't allowed to participate in the Lord's supper until becoming a church member. It didn't seem fair to be expected to support the offering with ten percent of my allowance but not be able to take communion.

As a child I didn't have the slightest notion what the communion was about. But I knew it was very special for my parents. Their devotion to the Lord's supper gave me a strong foundation for later appreciation, which I have today.

We talked a lot in Sunday school and at home about Jesus and his love for everybody. The communion made Jesus more present and real than words about him. I could touch him and he could touch me and everybody. I grew up in a little town near Ft. Worth, Texas. When I was a teenager I'd sit in the balcony during the worship service. There were some pretty tough men in our congregation, or so it seemed to me. They were ranchers and farmers with pickup trucks, frequently with a shotgun in the cab. Sometimes they would come to church from work with mud on their boots. When we had communion, they would come to the communion rail and actually kneel! I never saw those men kneel for *anything* else. It made a deep impression on me about the Lord's supper.

Would you like to have a great discussion in your church school class or in another suitable setting? Share your communion stories from your earliest memories. There will be joy, pathos, and humor.

Now here are some stories from later youth and adulthood.

Our task group of seven or eight adults from church was preparing to embark on our first prison visit. We had had several training sessions, but frankly, we were scared stiff. Before heading for the encounter with those in prison we gathered for a brief service of eucharist. I'll always remember that the biblical text was from the Matthew 25 Parable of the Last Judgment. "I was in prison and you visited me." Then we took bread and chalice following the words of Jesus from the Last Supper. We were still scared but less alone. From then on we never failed to have the sacrament prior to heading out for the prison.

Our son had returned home after a long stretch of drug addiction and alienation from the family. For the first time in years our family went to church together. It happened to be the first Sunday of the month, communion Sunday. I cannot tell you how deep an experience it was to kneel together and receive communion. We all cried at the kneeling rail and laughed about it later at home with thanksgiving in our hearts. It was like a certain biblical story. Our whole family had been lost and found again. At least we had a new beginning.

I attended an ecumenical Protestant service, the first of the kind for me. We concluded with a festive service of holy communion. I was like a wide-eyed child in a candy store. Never before had I been in a service with Presbyterians, Lutherans, Episcopalians, United Methodists, and members of the Disciples of Christ. It's been awhile now, so my memory is not sure whether there were still other denominations. There were people of different races and places, striking-looking banners, clergy in colorful attire, and others in everyday clothes. What I remember most vividly is how we all participated in the Lord's supper. Everyone was welcome. Isn't that the way our Lord meant it to be?

Our high school football team was favored to win the state championship. When we lost in the semi-finals, it was really devastating. Everything we had worked for went down the drain. I didn't feel like going to church the next day, but for some reason I did. We had communion. Don't ask me how or why, but somehow Jesus' sacrifice for us put things in a different perspective. The Saturday loss still hurt like everything. But it would be OK.

Some of my most cherished experiences of the Lord's supper have been in special times and places outside of the regular Sunday worship. I won't name them all, but here are a few examples: When we celebrated the dedication of our new home; at a retreat on a lake at sunset as part of a worship service, at the first meeting of the year for our church's new governing council. The Lord's supper has a way of bringing a special grace and acceptance. It sets the tone with Christ as host and guide.

Our pastor has trained several teams to take the communion to church members in the hospital, nursing homes, and those recuperating at home who are unable to attend Sunday services. We go in pairs to distribute the elements, which have been blessed in corporate worship. Let me tell you, it is a very moving experience. Several times my partner and I have offered communion to members with terminal illness. Cancer. AIDS. You name it. Sometimes they still have the strength to take bread and cup in their own hands. If not, we place the bread and wine on their lips if they can swallow. My life will never be the same.

To me the impact of the Lord's supper is related to the quality of personal relationships in a congregation. Our family has held membership in several congregations. One church was a closely knit people. There was a feeling of communion with each other over a period of time that made holy communion deeply meaningful. I guess I'm saying that the interaction of the people with the signs and sights of the sacrament is what's special.

The most memorable communions for me have been those connected with some special mission we were undertaking, either as a church or as a task group within the larger congregation. To experience Jesus in this way—the sacrament—is to take on the risks of his life.

I love the communion because at the table or altar of the Lord we are all welcome regardless of our status, our race, our nationality, our income, our sexual orientation, or anything else. There's nothing else quite like it.

My Own Eucharistic Journey

I grew up oblivious to the sacrament. I'm sure we observed monthly communion in the sanctuary, but I have absolutely no conscious remembrance of receiving the elements even after confirmation. As a school-aged child I was in worship regularly with my parents. My attendance as a teenager was more than respectable. What I do recall is listening intently to the sermons of Dr. Marshall T. Steel. They were understandable to a teenager and instrumental in shaping my vision of the church and its reason for being.

So I am with you if you grew up in the church and have, at best, a weak memory of the Lord's supper. Of course this condition says something about me as well as the church. How could I not recall taking communion, even if it didn't make any lasting impression in terms of meaning? Looking back with something close to 20-20 vision I'm aware, too, that the Lord's supper was nowhere near as important as preaching in the congregation in which I was baptized and confirmed.

My amnesia of the Lord's supper continued through my earliest young adult days and even through seminary. Vague memories of communion in the seminary chapel at Perkins School of Theology at Southern Methodist University are tucked away in my mind. Nothing of significance, however. The seminary has long since placed more emphasis on the sacrament both in the chapel and in classroom instruction.

There's an old saying that when the student is ready to learn, the teacher appears. I guess that I just wasn't ready to discern what for me has become a hidden depth of sacramental experience. An epiphany is more likely to happen if one is open to receiving it. This segment of my personal history provides me considerable understanding of other Christians who shake their heads in puzzlement at my passion for the eucharist. After all, one ought to be able to recognize one's former self. You already know that my hope is that *Eating and Drinking at the Welcome Table* can enrich your joy and blessing in eucharistic experience.

Discovery in the Local Church

My first awakening in relation to the Lord's supper began when I was pastor of St. Stephen Methodist Church in Mesquite, Texas. In 1959 the Bishop had appointed me to a vacant lot. The six-acre plot of ground was to become the future home of a new congregation. A three-week,1,700-door neighborhood survey found enough pioneers to cast their lot with a fledgling faith community. After what seemed like an eternity of holding worship services in an elementary school, the congregation moved into our new building.

Our rationale for worship space called for baptismal font, pulpit, and communion table of the same heavy oak material and equal visual prominence, yet all subordinate to a large cross of the same material. There was no structural separation between clergy and laity. For the Lord's supper the people came directly to the table to kneel and receive the elements. At that time we were using individual wafers and communion trays of individual cups.

Some time in the early 1960s a member of our worship committee suggested for the communion that we use a common loaf prepared by a member of the congregation. Today that might seem to be old hat, but for us at that time fresh bread was a fresh idea. You'd think we had never heard of 1 Corinthians 10:16–17: "The bread that we break, is it not a sharing in the body of Christ? Because there is one bread, we who are many are one body, for we all partake of the one bread."

For me, the common loaf was a wake-up call. The Lord's supper became more real, more earthy, yet more divine. More incarnational, more community oriented (we used a common chalice for the words of institution, even though we continued to use the individual cups for communion). Breaking and sharing the bread of Christ brought us closer to the brokenness of our own lives and the lives of our neighbors everywhere, yet closer to the healing present in the body of Christ. Somehow a common humanity knelt and rose from the table.

The common loaf evokes the hidden reality that we are a single fabric of hurting and hoping humanity. We belong to the common loaf and to each other. We belong to the one chalice which binds us together. These words, selected from a communion reflection called "For You and For You," by

Joy Jordan-Lake, a pastor and university teacher in Massachusetts, lift up the oneness of communion:

> We are about to engage in a strange, strange practice. Even the word we use for it is strange: communion. We don't really mean that, not most of the time, now do we? We're tough, self-reliant—wouldn't have made it this far, by golly, if we weren't…communion, indeed. With God, maybe—but only God, only as you and I personally conceive of God…
>
> Now and then the whole thing takes you by surprise, the words *This is my body, This is my blood* seeping quietly into and filling the hole inside you you'd forgotten was even there—if you ever knew it at all…
>
> There's another coming forward who feels within her another life, thumping and bumping and carving new caverns for itself beneath her ribs. And sometimes she finds herself startled by a kind of joy that tumbles, illogical, unbidden, altogether unreasonable, from somewhere deep within her.
>
> And she too hears *This is my body, This is my blood, for you.*
>
> There are others, though, who let their eyes wander discreetly around the room, see the face upon face upon face, and feel oddly cramped and crowded…and alone. Tired of being alone and tired of calling it all for the best and tired of concocting ecstatic remarks on other people's engagement rings and mustering up little cooing sounds for other people's babies and shaking hands eagerly with other people's parents in town for a visit. So tired of being cramped and crowded and all alone…And some others coming now have watched sickness come stalking, never fighting fair, watched mighty medical weapons crumple like cardboard swords, have watched and somehow managed still to hear *This is my body. This is my blood, shed for you…shed with you.*

Face upon face and life upon life, and you discover that what they say about how sharing pain lessens it is not quite true. Quite the opposite: her pain and his pain and their pain become your pain too—they weren't yours before. Somehow the pain becomes greater when it is passed around. But so does the healing. And so does the hope. And so does the joy.

This is my body, This is my blood.

Christ speaks among us and something peculiar happens: you and I and they, we are all marking our seven-year anniversary without a date; we are all approaching 95 and widowed; we are all getting married in July. We are all without the children we long for, have prayed for; we are all raising children who are handicapped, rebellious, precocious, impossible, delightful; we are all expecting a baby. We are all torn between tremendously flattering job offers in Singapore and San Diego; we are all on SSI, permanently unemployed. We are all planning on jogging the 20-mile Walk for Hunger; we are all facing major surgery.

We are many and we are one and we are happy and hurt and much in need of grace, of hearing *This is my body, this is my blood, for you.* (Jordan-Lake, 1996, 997–98)

The words. The common loaf of one Lord and one humanity. The people. A feast like no other feast. Sacramental seeds were growing in my life.

In 1967 I was appointed from St. Stephen to Northaven United Methodist Church across the Dallas metroplex. The practice at Northaven was and is for the people to form successive circles and receive the elements by intinction (dipping the bread into the chalice) while standing. The ordained clergy, assisted by laypersons, distribute the bread and the chalice to each person. This style of celebrating and administering the eucharist afforded me another discovery in my eucharistic journey.

Much of this book centers on meanings of *receiving* the eucharist. I began to discover at a deeper level during my pastorate at Northaven United Methodist Church what it can mean to be *giving* the bread and the cup. It had to do with two things. One was using a single cup or chalice for communion as well as a common loaf from which bread was broken. The elements themselves were a sign of community, of sharing together as a faith community. Secondly, it was a powerful and moving experience to look the receiving person in the eye and say, "This is the body of Jesus Christ broken for you, the blood of Christ shed for you," or similar words.

Why is this so? Because frequently I was privileged as a pastor to know something of the life situation of various church members. The struggles. The hopes. The crushing disappointments. Connecting their pain or brokenness or some newfound joy with the sheer gift of God's unconditional love in this embodied manner...well, it gets to me.

Here comes Joe (fictitious name but actual experience) to the front. He cups his hand to receive the bread. Our eyes meet. Earlier in the week this wealthy man with a pickup truck was driving to the edge of town to put his shotgun against his head. Somehow he lurched in a different direction and came to Northaven Church, driving almost blindly, yet with an unnamed compulsion. He managed to park in the church lot and come into the building.

I happened to be in the church study. He entered. He spoke. I didn't know what to say or do, except to listen. Anguish gushed forth. Grace embraced us both in ways far beyond my understanding. What do you think it was like, at least for me as his pastor, to say the words to Joe three days later in morning worship as we locked eyes: "Joe, this is Christ's body given for you." What an incredible privilege we pastors have to offer the bread and cup.

In one way or another Joe is multiplied a hundred times over. Here comes Jane to receive the elements. What is it like for her? She had a miscarriage two weeks ago. "This is the body of Christ for you. This is the blood of Christ." And now it's Mary's turn. She and Ralph had been married fifty-one years. He died last week after a long struggle with emphysema. Almost two years in a nursing home exhausted Mary emotionally, and it exhausted most of the savings for retirement. "This is the body and blood of Christ for you." The list goes on and on. You see the picture. At Northaven the eucharist and the human condition were forever wed in my mind and heart. I was hooked for life. Pain and grace. Brokenness and healing. Hurting and hoping. In its embodied way the eucharist enacts the old, old story.

One "special occasion" eucharist during my Northaven years bears telling. During the Vietnam War our congregation had the usual diverse opinions. After extensive study, research, and prayer I preached two sermons in September of 1967 in which I attempted to offer what I considered a prophetic voice. Years later people would sometimes ask, "Do you remember those five sermons you preached against the war?" (Maybe it seemed like five to the questioner.) As the war dragged on we decided to have an evening forum in which various opinions could be aired and discussed. We would conclude the evening with the eucharist.

Thirty-five church members showed up for the free-for-all discussion. There were so-called doves, hawks, and "I don't know what to think" participants. Two planned presentations were followed by discussion. Heat and light were both evident. Then with a few moments of silence as transition, we initiated the eucharist.

We sat in a single circle. I reminded the group of Wesley's sermon entitled "Catholic Spirit" in which he asks, "Though we cannot think alike, may we not love alike? May we not be of one heart, though we are not of one opinion?" Wesley replies, "Without all doubt, we may" (John Wesley 1944, 443–44). I offered the words of institution and a prayer for solidarity and healing. The bread and chalice were to be passed by the participants to each other around the circle, saying "The body and blood of Christ for you," or nothing at all if silence was more comfortable.

Two of the members who had opposite views of the war were seated next to each other. They had been a bit heated in their arguments. When Bob handed the bread to Harvey, he simply said, "Hang in there, Harvey." I thought to myself, "Well, not exactly the historic words of distribution, but nevertheless, words of grace!"

I'll always remember the *healing* brought by this eucharist. I'm not sure any other act of worship would have brought about the calm and the respect for each other across divided opinions. Reconciliation was acted out in the sharing of the Lord's body and blood, or as some would say, the Lord's embodied love for us all. Perhaps some of us have a sermonic phrase or image that has long been resident in our souls. Some of us also have memories of special eucharists attending us all of our days. For me this is one.

A Seminary Experience

By the time I left Northaven Church in 1973 to take on ministry at Saint Paul School of Theology, a United Methodist Seminary in Kansas City, Missouri, I was consciously aware of the significant place the eucharist had come to have in my faith. I had come a long way from growing up oblivious, but unknown to me there were still miles to go. During my days at Saint Paul I had what I have come to call my *mystical* experience of the eucharist. The word *mystery* is not foreign to my vocabulary. The very experience of grace is a mystery beyond the grasp of the most sophisticated thinker. But mystical? It seems to be the most fitting word for the following experience.

Chapel worship was held on Tuesdays and Thursdays at Saint Paul. As the school's president I made it a practice to attend as often as possible for the sake of my own faith and to set an example for students. Tuesday worship was usually a service of the Word and Thursday was word and table. One Thursday I was sitting near the back of the chapel. The bread and chalice on the communion table were uncovered. The sermon by a student preacher came and went. As time neared for the eucharistic liturgy, an unsettling yet compelling vision occurred in my experience. The communion table with the elements became superimposed on my desk in the president's office, so that the two became one, inseparably joined, an organic fusion. The elements now, as it were, rested on top of my communion table/office desk-become-one.

The bread and the chalice touched everything on my desk and everybody who entered the room. They touched the rough draft of my forthcoming report to the seminary's trustees. They touched the latest financial statement (which certainly needed something dramatic). They touched the inevitable government reports that give administrators ulcers and/or the blahs. Nothing escaped the embrace of the bread and wine. They touched the students, the maintenance staff, the faculty, the alums, the secretaries, indeed all who passed through the entrance to the president's office.

I don't know what else to say, except that I believe that after that experience I never administered the seminary in quite the same way. I don't know how to describe the difference. That's probably typical of the mystical. What I sensed was an imprint, an embodied paradigm, a sign and seal of a deeper disclosure and discernment. That's the best I can do with it in words. And part of me is glad I cannot do more with it in rational analysis. By now the eucharist had taken me just about all the way around the bases. It had become and remains central to the realities of faith, hope, and love.

A Coming Home Experience

After twelve years at Saint Paul School of Theology I accepted an invitation to return to Dallas as a faculty member at my alma mater, S.M.U.'s Perkins School of Theology. I was actually going to be paid to teach preaching and worship! My annual conference membership (United Methodist ecclesiology) had been moved in 1973 from the North Texas conference to the Missouri West Conference. It was time now—1985—to return to the North Texas Conference, a homecoming of sorts.

The closing worship service at the three-day Annual Conference session was a service of eucharist. I was excited.

Coming home. Old friends. Eucharist. A great combination. At the appropriate time I joined one of the lines going to the front to receive. Several clergy members were distributing the elements as we knelt at the communion railing. There was only one hitch, or so I thought. The serving elder before whom I was to kneel, as luck would have it, was a brother for whom I had very little respect. In my mind I said, "Lord, I've been gone for twelve years to the far country. This is my homecoming. Can't we do better than this?" Answer: "No." "Lord, do I have to receive your body and blood from *him*?" Answer: "Yes." So I knelt and received.

God's eucharist breaks through my narrow mind so that I'm given to understand the power and efficacy of the sacrament beyond human calculations or miscalculations.

In the early centuries of the church there was a group of North African schismatics known as the Donatists. They believed only good people could perform good sacraments. Augustine refuted this concept, claiming that the sacraments are not dependent upon the moral character of the celebrant but on God alone (White, *Intro*, 1990, 187–88). This is not to say in any form or fashion that the moral integrity of the clergy is less than a critical issue in the church. It is to say that if only perfect clergy or laity could administer the sacraments, there would be no sacraments. And there would certainly be no clergy.

So it was not seemingly bad luck that I was to kneel and receive the body and blood of Jesus Christ from a brother whom I had already judged. Would you say it was the grace and wisdom of God that countered my own self-righteousness and proved the wonders of God's love once again? Repentance and thanksgiving are all wrapped up in one another, don't you think? It was, in spite of myself, a marvelous homecoming.

On-the-Road Eucharists

Now let me relate three off-campus eucharists in which I participated during my years on the Perkins faculty...*way* off campus. In 1988 I participated in a ten-day educational

travel seminar to El Salvador and Nicaragua, sponsored by
the Center for Global Education, Augsburg College, Minneapolis. Our group of twelve came from several states. We
consisted of five clergy and seven laypersons, both female
and male. We were Lutheran, Disciples of Christ, Presbyterian, United Methodist, plus Roman Catholic staff members
in El Salvador and Nicaragua. Keep in mind that this was
during great turmoil and strife in both countries. We visited
with representatives of the conflicting parties in rural and
urban areas, as well as with various church leaders, campe-
sinos, and human rights representatives.

We were privileged to worship with the Maria Madre de
los Pobres (Mary Mother of the Poor) congregation in El Salvador in a structure built by the people. The work of this
faith community on the outskirts of San Salvador included
reading and interpreting the Bible on behalf of the reality of
the people; workshops in practical skills such as sewing; lay
leadership for better health, housing, and literacy. Anyone
organizing for decent living conditions was considered subversive by the treasury police. Four of the police appeared at
the Sunday service with automatic weapons. Through an
interpreter, the laypeople told our group, "Those who meet
to discuss the Word of God are watched. Terrorizing people
is constant. Sometimes as a result of commitment to evange-
lization you can disappear and end up in a trash dump. We
are called agitators and subversives."

In this environment the worship took place. The service
was vital and lively, including music, a homily by Fr. Daniel
Sanchez, passing of the peace, and eucharist. The passing of
the peace is an experience of great exuberance. Strangers received warm hugs. Everyone was welcome to participate in
the bread and wine. Could it have been nine years ago? It
seems like yesterday, still vivid in my mind's eye. For these
brothers and sisters of meager worldly resources and abundant courage under constant threat, the eucharist is a great
feast of the liberating Lord, joyful, celebrative, for us gringos
an unforgettable experience. In my judgment their feast was

a paradigm of what the Lord meant for the occasion to be. But more about that in the succeeding chapters.

Traveling through Nicaragua was also a learning experience. Our group exhausted notebooks and pens taking notes from many sessions of listening and inquiry. At one session in Matagalpa we were sitting on three benches in a row in a small room, trying to understand agrarian land reform. The image of "back to school" stuck in my mind. It's not a bad image for North Americans in relation to Latin America.

Our group's final evening in Managua, the last stop on the trip, brought a time of reflection as we lifted our hearts to God and each other. Everyone contributed to the homily, consummated with a makeshift table, a loaf of bread, and a chalice of wine. For ten days we had shared laughter, tears, arguments, anxiety, bone-tiredness, meals, turista, and back-to-school learning. We had received the unforgettable hospitality of people who had the barest physical necessities, people who fed us with food, including the food of a remarkable faith. So following a rough approximation of a brief prayer of Great Thanksgiving, we broke bread and drank wine, offering the elements to each other. There are some eucharists one always remembers.

A eucharist in a completely different on-the-road setting occurred in a Swiss Reformed Church some years ago. I was in the small town of Château D'Oex in the French section of Switzerland. I knew no one. I don't speak French. An alien world for me? Yes and no. Yes because I was a stranger and ignorant for the most part of the language. No because of familiar symbols, colors, and liturgical acts. The homily passed over my head. When it came time for the eucharist, children came forward with a beautiful array of flowers. The music made me feel at home. Unlike the usual practice at Reformed Churches in the United States, the people began to rise, go forward, and form a circle around the table. I was accustomed to this kind of movement.

I went forward with those sitting in my pew. Adults and children circled the table. The celebrant brought bread to each person. To my complete surprise *two* chalices followed. I figured out that one was wine and the other non-alcoholic. Presumably the latter was for children and any adults who for their own reasons would opt for the unfermented fruit of the vine. Never before had I seen this eucharistic option. United Methodists don't ordinarily have this choice.

Why do I recall this eucharist with special gratitude? For the odd-sounding reason that I didn't know anyone or comprehend the language. While I would not choose an unfamiliar setting on a regular basis, it conveyed yet another dimension of the eucharist. The global and timeless quality of the eucharist was brought home to me in a most memorable way. The sacrament was not dependent on familiar surroundings, understandable language, an accompanying group, or customary practices. The faith of the people, the liturgical movement, and the act of receiving the elements interacted to communicate the presence of the eternal, global reality of God and one segment of God's people. Beyond language, beyond culture, beyond nationality, yet particularized within each language, culture, and nationality. A sacrament for all seasons and all times and all places.

Meanwhile, Back to Your Eucharistic Journey

My fervent hope is for the enrichment of *your* thoughts and experiences of the eucharist through the sharing of mine and others. This could happen in several ways: (1) you could look back on your past experience with new eyes and ears; (2) you might look forward to future eucharists with either reinforced or brand new expectations; (3) you might find that sharing viewpoints with others may seem more likely to reveal deeper meanings. Tell the story. Listen to the story. Give thanks for the spread of the welcome table.

3

The Eucharist as Personal and Pastoral

Christians have understood the eucharist in a variety of ways. Indeed, to reduce what Christians experience in the eucharist to a single interpretation would be to miss much of the eucharist's power.

White, 1990, 239

What does the Lord's supper mean to you? Is there a core or single experience prominent for you, such as thanksgiving or confession? Or might there be several meanings that vary according to your life circumstances? How and from whom has your understanding of the eucharist developed? While the eucharist is first and last a corporate reality as a sacrament *of the church*, it cannot be separated from the meaning experienced by each worshiper in the context of that person's life.

Through the centuries, Christians have described their eucharistic experiences in multiple ways. Theologians of the church have likewise offered several interpretations. The namings by rank-and-file Christians and by scholars actually coincide to provide basically the same overall set of interpretations. This chapter will explore these meanings. In addition I will indicate some ways of talking about the eucharist from my own experience that "get inside" some of these historic interpretations.

For centuries the eucharist has been a source for renewing and centering the personal faith of Christians. This is what I mean by eucharist as deeply personal and pastoral. Of course the personal and the prophetic cannot be separated, whether in sacramentality or in other forms of pastoral care. Personal well-being and community well-being belong together in any biblical approach to Christian faith. Thus I invite you to regard this chapter and chapter 4 (eucharist as public and prophetic) as a unified continuum. After all, holy communion is a gift of God, centered in Jesus Christ, intended to nurture and empower our baptism, that is, our identity in Christ and our ministry to the world in Christ's name.

As you read and consider these various ways of describing the eucharist, see how they relate to and inform your experiences and those of your worshiping community.

Joyful Thanksgiving/Thankful Praise

The theme of thanksgiving has long been associated with the Lord's supper, especially in the earliest practice of the church. Blessing the bread and giving thanks over the cup are clearly associated with the upper room meal with roots from the Jewish prayer tradition. The eucharistic theme links Christians with the Jewish *berakah*, the blessing and praise of God. In Acts 2:46 we read "They broke bread at home and ate their food with glad and generous hearts, praising God and having the goodwill of all the people." Keep in mind that the practice of a meal centered in joyful thanksgiving to God had been going on for perhaps twenty years prior to the writing of the first New Testament books.

Thanksgiving in relation to the Lord's supper comes from the Greek verb *eucharisteo*, adapted as "eucharist" in English. It seems worth noting that the word eucharist comes from the root *charis*, meaning grace, favor, gratitude. From *charis* comes "charisma" or "gift." *Eucharisteo* is used in each of the synoptic gospel accounts of the Last Supper (Matthew 26:27; Mark 14:23; and Luke 22:17, 19) as well as in Paul's First Corinthians account of the Last Supper (11:24). The recurring use of eucharisteo provides clear evidence in the New Testament for joyful thanksgiving to God as a theme for this sacrament—thanksgiving for God's liberating love in Jesus Christ and for God's mighty action in creation and covenant-making. The term eucharisteo was so prominent in instituting the Last Supper that eucharist became a basic term for describing or including other meanings for the sacrament as well.

In his book *The Great Thanksgiving* Keith Watkins provides yet a broader view of eucharist: "A useful English equivalent to *eucharisteo* is *thankful praise*, which can also describe the general quality of the Christian life and the specifically religious act of holy communion. Christian worship is the constant offering of prayer to God; and the ceremonies with bread and wine, remembering Jesus Christ, are the distinctive vehicle by which the churches express their great thanksgiving" (Watkins 1995, 4).

In a section of the Preface entitled "A Word about Words" I suggested that different primary terms for the sacrament used by various church bodies nevertheless carry a common meaning. Whether we say eucharist or holy communion or the Lord's supper, joyful thanksgiving or thankful praise is shared by all as one of the meanings of this earliest of Christian practices.

Our participation in the sacrament, then, can be an occasion of profound gratitude for God's goodness, a time of praising God for blessings taken for granted, an encounter in which we recover our true life once again as recipients of God's irrepressible grace.

Jesus gave thanks. Our earliest faith forebears gave thanks. Christians in all ages have given thanks. We give thanks. Our children's children will give thanks.

Commemoration/Remembrance

"This is my body that is for you. Do this in remembrance of me...This cup is the new covenant in my blood. Do this, as often as you drink it, in remembrance of me." How many millions of Christians through the centuries have heard these or similar words in preparation for the Lord's supper? Paul's words in 1 Corinthians (11:23–25) are part of the earliest tradition he delivers to the church. Paul uses the Greek word *anamnesis* for "remembrance." This remembrance is intended to be similar to the Passover remembrance, that is, in a way which makes contemporary and present the promise and claim of a past event. An apt analogy might be the intent of preaching, where the gift and demand of God through Jesus Christ is made current for today's listener. Remembering in this visible, visceral way with the partaking of bread and wine is done so that the story, so to speak, will happen again. Elie Wiesel, known to many as a Holocaust theologian and author, once said that he had dedicated his life to remembering. We Christians do well to dedicate our lives to remembering the Christ of compassion and justice. The Christ who did not fail to remember the outcast and the dispossessed. To be continually *restored* we need to be *restoried*.

Anamnesis is the opposite of amnesia. The eucharist as remembrance is a field day for the imagination. Jesus Christ becomes present in many scenes of the mind so as to be present in the here and now. Perhaps we remember other examples of his table fellowship, then and now. His welcoming of the sinner, then and now. His affirmation of the Samaritan woman, then and now. His love for children, then and now. His lifting the lowly and lowering the lofty, then and now. Mary. Andrew. The man born blind. Peter. The woman bent over for eighteen years. All then. And all now. We don't remember just anyone: We remember the vulnerable, victorious One who by the power of the Holy Spirit is always now as well as then. No mere memorial is this. In the sacrament the Presence is present.

So whether we come forward to receive Jesus Christ or we receive him where we already are, we are already remembered by the One whom we will be remembering.

Communion/Koinonia

"I look forward to the Lord's supper because it is an experience of Christian community and sharing at a very deep level." This often-heard comment reflects a meaning of the sacrament very dear to many hearts. The sixteenth-century Protestant Reformation reclaimed this emphasis on congregational fellowship through lay participation, simpler rites, and the language of the people.

Once again we return to Paul's 1 Corinthians. In 10:16–17 he writes: "The cup of blessing that we bless, is it not a sharing in the blood of Christ? The bread that we break, is it not a sharing in the body of Christ? Because there is one bread, we who are many are one body, for we all partake of the one bread." The *Revised Standard Version* uses the term *participation*, whereas the NRSV uses *sharing*. Paul uses the term *koinonia*. The word can be used for participation, sharing, or fellowship.

As James White reminds us, "The unity given here is not just human conviviality: it is a gift given in the breaking of bread, a sharing in the body of Christ. It builds upon the Jewish understanding that a meal binds together participants" (White, *Sacrament* 1983, 56). The oneness in baptism is reenacted, celebrating oneness with church and with each other, as well as oneness in service to the world.

To participate or share (*koinonia*) in the eucharist is to be bound together with Christians throughout time and throughout the world. You might not understand the spoken word of worship in France or El Salvador or Hong Kong or Kenya. But the eucharist in whatever language and form will bring you to the upper room and the village of Emmaus in the Body of Christ with other worshiping Christians.

Sacrifice/Self-Giving

The word sacrifice is basic to the Christian story, yet for many persons it carries questionable connotations. I like the term "self-giving" used by James White. The life, death, and resurrection of Jesus is certainly summarized as a self-giving to others, that is, a way of life characterized by love of God and love of neighbor. Self-giving seems to denote a way of life freely and intentionally chosen in the footsteps of Jesus Christ on behalf of others. What would life be without the self-giving, or sacrifice if you like, of parents for children, between husband and wife, of friends for each other? Jesus' Sermon on the Mount ethic would also include sacrifice or self-giving for one's enemies: "Love your enemies and pray for those who persecute you" (Matthew 5:44).

Unfortunately, the seemingly Christian-approved notion of sacrifice is misused by persons and systems of power against the relatively powerless. All too often Christian sacrifice can be made to sound like and be like a form of servitude or servility instead of genuine service. A clear statement of this dilemma is offered by Marjorie Procter-Smith in her book *In Her Own Rite*:

> Sacrifice is a profound expression of solidarity when undertaken voluntarily or on behalf of someone else. It fails to carry the same message when forced on those who are already expected to have nothing. As with the image of servant for those who are regarded as natural servants, the idea of sacrifice carries no transformative message for those, like women, who are expected to be sacrificial by nature. (Procter-Smith 1990, 161)

Since the whole ministry of Christ abounds with sacrificial images, what are we to conclude? In regard to the eucharist we read and hear of covenant blood poured out for many (Matthew 26:27–28). Or "This cup is the new covenant in my blood" (1 Corinthians 11:25). Is Christ's example of sacrifice a danger in a society with huge power differentials, or a supreme example for Christians to follow and a necessary leavening factor in a world starved for goodwill? Surely it is both, depending on how it is interpreted and implemented.

Again the insight of Marjorie Procter-Smith is instructive:

> However, two things may be said of the sacrifice demanded by an emancipatory eucharist. First, the sacrifice is, as the eucharist is, a communal rather than an

individual act. The whole community of the church is called upon to sacrifice on behalf of the poorest women of the world. Second, sacrifice must aid the struggle of women for survival and dignity. Those who benefit from the oppression of women are called upon to sacrifice their privilege where it will benefit women. Since some women are also in some ways beneficiaries of not only sexism but also racism and classism, we too are called upon to sacrifice our privilege where it will benefit the struggle of women in general. The ability to offer such sacrifice demands a high degree of discernment and the knowledge of intersecting oppressions. It also demands an understanding of the ways in which a patriarchal ideology of sacrifice has sustained sexism and racism. This is particularly critical for women, who have often been called upon to sacrifice ourselves, or have been sacrificed against our wills. (Procter-Smith 1990, 161)

At its best, sacrifice as a eucharistic theme embraces us with the unmerited grace of God's self-giving and the corresponding call for us to be caring and compassionate neighbors, the body of Christ for others. I can give no better counsel in this chapter's section on the sacrament's sacrificial theme than to recommend some time spent with your church's hymnal. You will discover some rich images of the eucharist you've sung many times and perhaps some new ones as well. Consider these poetic words from the hymnal I know best:

Come, sinners, to the Gospel feast, let every soul be
    Jesus' guest.
Ye need not one be left behind, for God hath bid all
    humankind.
See him set forth before your eyes; behold the bleed
    ing sacrifice;
his offered love make haste to embrace, and freely
    now be saved by grace.
            (Charles Wesley, in *The United Methodist Hymnal*)
                                                    1989, 616

I come with joy to meet the Lord, forgiven, loved and
    free,
in awe and wonder to recall his life laid down for me,
    his life laid down for me.

                                   (Brian Wren, in *UMH* 1989, 617)

Now let us from this table rise renewed in body,
    mind, and soul;
with Christ we die and live again, his selfless love has
    made us whole.

                                   (Fred Kaan, in *UMH* 1989, 634)

Christ's Presence

Christ's presence in the eucharist has been articulated
and experienced in many ways by Christians through the
centuries. Like Charles Wesley's hymn "O the Depths of Love
Divine," many Christians are more likely to speak of the *experience* of Christ's presence than the *how* of his presence.

O the depth of love divine, the unfathomable grace!
Who shall say how bread and wine God into us
    conveys!
How the bread his flesh imparts, how the wine
    transmits his blood,
fills his faithful people's hearts with all the life of
    God!
Sure and real is the grace, the manner be unknown;
only meet us in thy ways and perfect us in one.
Let us taste the heavenly powers, Lord, we ask for
    nothing more.
Thine to bless, 'tis only ours to wonder and adore.

                                   (Charles Wesley, in *UMH* 1989, 627)

These words may not satisfy the arguments of some theologians, but I expect they speak for many Christians. "Sure
and real is the grace," as Charles Wesley states, a grace that
"fills his faithful people's hearts with all the life of God."
Whether we prefer to speak of Christ's real presence or

spiritual presence in the sacrament, the grace of that presence is real to faith.

I have no hesitancy in speaking of the real presence of God in Jesus Christ in the eucharist. I mean that the promise and claim of God's gospel in Jesus Christ is as surely present to faith as in the upper room or the Emmaus experience. I find this functional or action-oriented description of Christ's presence in the sacrament more satisfactory than the more substance- and spatial-oriented interpretation rooted in Aristotelian and medieval philosophy. To me Christ is truly present in the entire sacramental experience…in the bread and wine, in the gathered community of faith, in the liturgical interaction of God and people. Today both Roman Catholic and Protestant theologians are exploring various ways to articulate Christ's presence in the eucharist.

Thus far in this chapter five New Testament images or meanings of the eucharist have been lifted up. They represent a convergence of experience expressed by Christians over the years with the writing of Yngve Brilioth, the former Lutheran archbishop of Uppsala, Sweden (Brilioth 1961, 1–69).

A Foretaste of the Messianic Banquet

"For as often as you eat this bread and drink the cup, you proclaim the Lord's death until he comes" (1 Corinthians 11:26). In Mark 14:25 are these words: "Truly I tell you, I will never again drink of the fruit of the vine until that day when I drink it new in the kingdom of God." Similar words of Jesus to his disciples in the upper room occur in Matthew 26:29 and Luke 22:16. What are we to make of these statements?

They remind us that God's work in the world is unfinished and has a future dimension. Worshipers sometimes say after receiving the communion, "This is the way God meant it to be: everyone equal and in communion with God and each other; no distinctions of race, class, gender, sexual orientation, or status." The eucharist, then, is an expression of yearning, of hope for God's victory over every barrier separating life from God and life from life. The concluding prayer in one of the eucharistic services goes like this:

> By your spirit make us one with Christ, one with each
>   other, and one in ministry to all the world, until
> Christ comes in final victory and we feast at his
>   heavenly banquet. *(UMH* 1989, 11)

A United Church of Canada prayer offers this vision:

> Therefore, as we eat this bread and drink this cup,
> we are proclaiming Christ's death until he comes.
> In the body broken and the blood poured out,
> we restore memory and hope
> of the broken and unremembered victims
> of tyranny and sin;
> and we long for the bread of tomorrow
> and the wine of the age to come.
> Come then, life-giving spirit of our God,
> brood over these bodily things,
> and make us one body with Christ,
> that we may labour with creation
> to be delivered from its bondage to decay
> into the glorious liberty
> of all the children of God.
> Amen. *(Voices United* 1996–97, 51)

Confession and Repentance

Has the theme of penitence been misplaced or forgotten? Many Christians have grown up on a sacramental diet of guilt and contrition. Indeed, depending on one's experience, the emphasis of bewailing "our manifold sins and wickedness...most grievously committed" is often the first thought regarding the meaning of holy communion.

So as to leave no doubt in your mind I want to state unequivocally that I regard confession and repentance as fundamental to the church's understanding of the gospel and of life itself. There can be no new future apart from the practice of reevaluation, self-reflection, and the principle of change. This is true for individuals, for groups, and certainly for the church itself. Regular worship without confession and pardon is simply a form of self-deception.

During the fifteen years of my pastorates, confession was the first order of business in Sunday services—following the call to worship, opening hymn, and perhaps a brief collect or prayer. During all those years the Methodist Church communion service was rooted in the lineage of Wesley-Cranmer (Anglican Archbishop and key influence on the Book of Common Prayer)—that is, in medieval Roman Catholicism. *Translation*: heavy on the penitential, and I mean heavy. In between numerous "have mercy" statements were sandwiched offers of pardon and further statements of our manifold sins and wickedness. The prayer of humble access included, "We are not worthy so much as to gather up the crumbs under thy table."

Now comes the eye opener, at least for me. The *emphasis* on the penitential is virtually absent in New Testament images of the eucharist, as well as in the eucharist of the early church. One exception is Jesus' statement in Matthew: "Drink from it, all of you; for this is my blood of the covenant, which is poured out for many for the forgiveness of sins" (Matthew 26:27–28). We've already seen in chapter 1 excerpts from the second-century service reported by Justin Martyr. In chapter 7 we will examine briefly liturgies of the early church and compare them with other services. Nowhere in Brilioth's New Testament images of the eucharist is there emphasis on the penitential. Apparently the early church believed that the eucharist was above all a gift to sinners rather than a penitential critique of the human condition.

Over a long period of time a strong penitential piety with its focus on human guilt took firm rootage in the church. By the thirteenth century the sacrament of penance was required for Easter communion. The ground was thus prepared for a penitential view of communion with its focus on moral fitness as a condition for participation. In spite of many changes in the sacramental system brought about by the Protestant Reformation, the medieval penitential piety remained substantially in place:

> When the sacrament of penance was abolished...the result was to push the eucharist into being a penitential sacrament too, a process already strongly developed in late medieval piety. Ever since the Reformation, the Protestant eucharist has done double duty as a sacrament both of penance and of thanksgiving...it simply overloaded the eucharist. (White, *Introduction*, 1990, 180)

Perhaps the eucharist is perfectly capable of combining several emphases, because human experience is not neatly separated into compartments. William B. McClain combines festive celebration with repentance as he describes the eucharist in the black church. The black church, he says, experiences the eucharist as a festive celebration of Christ overcoming death, not as a funeral or even a memorial of utter solemnity. Not a Good Friday, but an Easter Sunday with a gift of grace calling forth commitment.

> The celebration of communion is a party for prodigals who have fallen on their knees, some in the swine pens away from home, some who have wallowed in smugness and self-righteousness at home, but all can come back to take a seat at the place that has been saved for them at the banquet table. (McClain 1997, 11)

The welcome table is a scene of both repentance and thanksgiving. Many Christians do experience the eucharist as a time for reassessment, for a new beginning placed in the hands of the table Host or laid upon the altar of God. Should not repentance and pardon be accompanied by celebration and thanksgiving? And is there not joy in heaven?

The variety of eucharistic understanding and interpretations explored in this chapter come from New Testament images, the long tradition of the church, and contemporary experience. Without doubt other ways of naming our experiences can be added. Human experience is not easily limited or categorized! Here are some additional terms which I have heard through the years: a healing experience; a reconciling sacrament; a nurturing, sustaining event; a mystery of union and unity beyond the human intellect.

Personal Reflections

I find the eucharist to be a very moving experience and at times overpowering. The bread and wine have a way of uncovering the source of my life: sheer gift, pure grace. Simultaneously, everything is perfectly clarified and everything is a complete mystery. All pretenses are exposed, strategies of control stripped away. The eucharist seems to lift up every act of self-giving, every deed of love in the history of the universe. It points to all that is good and re-creating in life, all that offers hope in spite of every in spite of.

I like to receive the eucharist with hands overlapping with palms up. This is a gesture of letting go and receiving. Let go of the trivial, the false, the hurtful. Receive the profound, the eternal, the true, the demanding. A story about the Greek novelist Nikos Kazantzakis helps me discern eucharistic meaning for my life:

> The novelist was on a remote island visiting a saintly monk and asked him, "Do you still wrestle with the devil, Fr. Makarios?" The monk replied, "Not any longer, my child. I have grown old and the devil has grown old with me. He doesn't have the strength. I now wrestle with God." "With *God*? exclaimed Kazantzakis. "And you hope to win?" "No," the monk replied, "I hope to lose." (Toohey 1980, 29–30)

Eucharist as joyful thanksgiving and thankful praise? How could it not be? Countless blessings come to the surface with a life of their own, totally undeserved. Commemoration and remembrance? Of course. I receive not just anybody's body and blood, but that of a Jew, a refugee, a lowly carpenter who told stories of Samaritans, both female and male as examples, himself an outcast among outcasts.

Communion/*Koinonia*? One body in Christ, all seekers in the hands of a loving God. Rejoice with those who rejoice. Weep with those who weep. Communion alone is a contradiction in terms, except in unusual circumstances. Sacrifice/self-giving? I am who I am only through the self-giving of others, a fact of life grounded in Jesus Christ.

Christ's presence? Yes, in countless ways, but especially focused in the visible sacrament. A foretaste of the messianic banquet? The eucharist is an act of hope—hope that life is moving from God, with God, and toward God. Confession and repentance? When I am overwhelmed with gratitude, a spirit of humility surfaces, bringing the realization that I have "taken great benefits with little thanks" (*The Book of Worship for Church and Home* 1964, 385).

For me the eucharist is like a great tapestry of life with intersecting, interacting fabrics. Thanksgiving and repentance belong to each other. Christ's presence is known in koinonia. In communion with one another the living Christ is there, as he promised. Christ is present through remembering. In remembering him we are led to praise and confession. On any given eucharistic celebration one of these fabrics might come front and center according to the fabric of life lived during the preceding week.

One of the recurring experiences in the Lord's supper for me is what I now call a reversal of the "Why me?" We ordinarily use Why me? in the negative sense. Why did this or that happen to me or us? Sometimes I ask it almost unthinkingly because my self-deception of being in control is shattered. Nothing serious: My plans just didn't work out. Sometimes it's more serious: a sick family member, an operation. Why us?

The eucharist brings a contrasting vision, embracing me with God's unmerited love, saving me from myself. I am led to ask in wonder and gratitude, "Why me, Lord? Why do I have enough to eat when so many in the world do not? Why do I have shelter and clothing, and why have I enjoyed good health for so many years when others are in great pain? Why me, Lord? Why did I have loving parents I did not choose?" The liberating love of God reverses the Why me, Lord? and becomes the invitation and motivation out of gratitude to feed the hungry, to welcome the stranger, and to clothe the naked. In other words, the eucharist keeps pointing me beyond myself to God's action in the world.

There is a second dimension to the "Why me?" for oppressed peoples, battered women, and those rejected due to race, class, gender, or sexual orientation. The eucharist invites an awareness of "Why me?" that lifts the lowly and lowers the lofty in ways similar to the Magnificat. "Why should I be relegated to nobodiness by others, to second-class citizenship? Why me, Lord? Why should I be put down and dismissed? Your love embodied in the sacrament lifts my sense of self-worth and my determination through your grace to break through the conceptual traps designed for me by the dominant culture. Your love in the sacrament frees me to free others as your agent of compassion and justice."

The gift of the eucharist, wisely discerned, is God's way of welcoming us and feeding us according to our particular need and circumstance. I don't know how God knows what we need most in terms of the gospel. Comfort? Challenge? Restored eyesight? Fresh ears? God knows, somehow.

The eucharist is much too rich in meaning to be limited to a somber memorial. The welcome table must always begin with the upper room where, on the night in which he gave himself up for us, Jesus took bread and cup, gave thanks to God, broke the bread and poured the cup, and offered himself to his disciples. But the self-giving didn't stop there. As we see in the Luke 24 Emmaus account of the Risen Christ with his disciples, *the Last Supper has become the Everlasting Supper*, an eternal reminder of God's unconditional love and thus an occasion of joyful celebration. This is a table to be spread far and wide with a feast of love, peace, and justice in concert with all like-minded souls. We turn now in that direction.

4

The Eucharist as Public and Prophetic

The eucharist has been domesticated within the dominant social establishment of the day. Its radical demands have been largely neutralized. (Balasuriya 1979, xi)

When you have partaken of this sacrament, therefore, or desire to partake of it, you must in turn share the misfortunes of the fellowship...all the unjust suffering of the innocent, with which the world is everywhere filled to overflowing. You must fight, work, pray, and—if you cannot do more—have heartfelt sympathy. (Luther 1519)

The eucharistic celebration...is a constant challenge in the search for appropriate relationships in social, economic and political life...All kinds of injustice, racism, separation and lack of freedom are radically challenged when we share in the body and blood of Christ. (Henderson, Larson and Quinn 1989, 101)

I believe the public and prophetic meanings of the eucharist may well be the best-kept secret in the North American church. Rarely if ever have I heard worshiping Christians give even lip service to this dimension of the sacrament. In the previous chapter we looked at various eucharistic meanings which were enumerated by Yngve Brilioth, the former Swedish archbishop of Uppsala. The prophetic implications are nowhere to be found in his New Testament images of early eucharistic practice. Perhaps the prophetic implications are more implied than explicitly named, yet there can be no doubt that the Christian movement was seen as subversive to Rome and the authority of the emperor.

While there are numerous publications on liturgy and justice, there seems to be a dearth of literature specifically on eucharist and justice. This is especially true in Protestant writings where the relation between eucharist and public life appear to me to be undeveloped if not conspicuously absent. My hope is that this chapter will be a contribution to the literature and to your understanding and experience of the eucharist.

The Source of Justice

God's justice is rooted in the very character of God and is expected to be reflected in the life of God's people (Birch 1991). The scriptures point to God as the source of justice. A few examples mentioned here could easily be joined by a whole symphony of other texts. This section will enumerate some of the signs of justice, although the biblical texts themselves will do this on their own.

Talk with Moses and Pharaoh. They can tell us more about God as the source of justice than oppressors in any culture and age want to know. Burning bush, God's liberating mission, reluctant Moses, "Let my people go," resistance, plagues to free the slaves, the Lord's Passover, an economic and political system of oppression collapsing like a cardboard house. Would Moses, a solitary sheep-herding, fugitive murderer from Egypt have dreamed this up? Against Pharaoh's armies? Justice is from God.

Justice from the heart and soul of God is easily identified in the law, the psalms, and the prophets. Numerous passages in Deuteronomy and Leviticus call for protection of the poor. "The LORD your God...executes justice for the orphan and the widow and...loves the strangers [*sojourners* in RSV], providing them food and clothing" (Deuteronomy 10:18).

God's justice is a plentiful theme in Psalms. One of my favorites for years has been Psalm 82 in which God (Yahweh) brings judgment to the council of gods because they are not doing their job. Their job is to give justice to the weak and the orphan, to maintain the rights of the lowly and the destitute, to rescue the weak and the needy, and to deliver them from the hand of the wicked (Psalm 82:3–4). In Psalm 72 a prayer is offered for guidance and support for the king: "Give the king your justice, O God, and your righteousness to a king's son. May he judge your people with righteousness, and your poor with justice...May he defend the cause of the poor of the people, give deliverance to the needy, and crush the oppressor" (vv. 1–2, 4–5).

From Psalm 89: "Righteousness and justice are the foundation of your throne; steadfast love and faithfulness go before you" (v. 14). A well-known psalm of thanksgiving for God's goodness begins with "Bless the Lord, O my soul" (103:1) and proceeds from the personal to the public and prophetic: "The Lord works vindication and justice for all who are oppressed. He made known his ways to Moses, his acts to the people of Israel" (vv. 6–7). The latter verses, of course, refer to the exodus event, a central point of reference for much of the Psalter.

Then there are themes of justice in the tradition of Israel's prophets. Probably the most memorable statement is from Micah: "What does the Lord require of you but to do justice, and to love kindness, and to walk humbly with your God?" (6:8). And from Amos, in his scathing denunciation of worship that is disconnected from justice:

> I hate, I despise your festivals,
>   and I take no delight in your
>   solemn assemblies.

> Even though you offer me your
>   burnt offerings and grain
>   offerings,
>   I will not accept them;
> and the offerings of well-being
>   of your fatted animals
>   I will not look upon.
> Take away from me the noise of
>   your songs;
>   I will not listen to the melody
>   of your harps.
> But let justice roll down like waters,
>   and righteousness like an
>   everflowing stream.
>   Amos 5:21–24

The prophet Isaiah likewise offers a pointed message from God concerning Israel's worship. Following their return from exile the people are without a sense of direction. The nation languishes in gloom. So the people humble themselves through fasting, in sackcloth and ashes, hoping to gain Yahweh's favor. They are puzzled, even complaining, when Yahweh pays no attention. Yahweh's reply:

> Is not this the fast that I choose:
>   to loose the bonds of injustice,
>   to undo the thongs of the yoke,
>   to let the oppressed go free,
>   and to break every yoke?
> Is it not to·share your bread with
>   the hungry,
>   and bring the homeless poor
>   into your house;
>   when you see the naked, to
>   cover them,
>   and not to hide yourself from
>   your own kin?

Then your light shall break forth
     like the dawn,
  and your healing shall spring
     up quickly;
your vindicator shall go before you,

   the glory of the Lord shall be
     your rear guard.
Then you shall call, and the
     Lord will answer;
you shall cry for help, and he
     will say, Here I am.

If you remove the yoke from
     among you,
  the pointing of the finger,
     the speaking of evil,
if you offer your food to the hungry
  and satisfy the needs of the afflicted,
then your light shall rise in the darkness
  and your gloom be like
     the noonday

The Lord will guide you continually,
  and satisfy your needs
     in parched places,
  and make your bones strong;
and you shall be like a watered garden,
  like a spring of water,
  whose waters never fail.
Your ancient ruins shall be rebuilt;
  you shall raise up the
     foundations of many generations;
you shall be called the repairer
     of the breach,
  the restorer of streets to live in.
                    Isaiah 58:6–12

Yahweh's reinterpretation of Israel's worship calls for a major re-imaging of Israel's' worship or fast from an ascetic act to an ethical act. The emphasis shifts from self-absorption to solidarity with the outcast and the oppressed.

Is our worship today expressive of the twin goals of personal transformation and doing justice?

The New Testament continues the theme of justice. Jesus consistently speaks and acts in ways that support the worth and dignity of all people, especially those disregarded by religious and political authorities. The central focus of Jesus' teachings is the Kingdom or Rule of God. An insightful study of the gift, hope, and challenge of the Reign of God is provided by Mortimer Arias in *Announcing the Reign of God:*

> The kingdom of God, announced by Jesus, is multidimensional and all-encompassing. It is both a present and a future reality. It has to do with each individual creature and with the whole of society. It was addressed initially to "the lost sheep of the house of Israel," but was destined for "the whole world" and to "the end of the earth." It embraces all dimensions of human life: physical, spiritual, personal and interpersonal, communal and societal, historical and eternal. And it encompasses all human relationships—with the neighbor, with nature, and with God. It implies a total offer and a total demand. Everything and everybody has to be in line with it: "Turn away from your sins and believe the Good News" (Mark 1:15, TEV) of the kingdom of God. (Luke 11:42 and Matthew 23:23). (Arias 1984, xv)

God's rule is a message of justice, a reality for which we pray on a regular basis in the Lord's Prayer. Do we realize what we are saying when we pray for God's kingdom to come on earth? We are praying for a revolution to occur, a radical change in a world of violence and unimaginable disparity between rich and poor. Should we pray for change unless we are willing for God to shape our lives accordingly?

Jesus' prophetic message of justice is pronounced in a very specific way: "Woe to you, scribes and Pharisees, hypocrites! For you tithe mint, dill, and cummin, and have neglected the weightier matters of the law: justice and mercy and faith. It is these you ought to have practiced, without neglecting the others." (Matthew 23:23) In Matthew 12 Jesus is portrayed as fulfilling the words of the prophet Isaiah: "Here is my servant, whom I have chosen, my beloved, with whom my soul is well pleased. I will put my Spirit upon him, and he will proclaim justice to the Gentiles...He will not break a bruised reed or quench a smoldering wick until he brings justice to victory. And in his name the Gentiles will hope" (18, 20–21, from Isaiah 42:1–4).

Many other New Testament passages allude to the theme of justice as fundamental to God's covenant relationship with the Christian community just as it continued to be with Israel in the Hebrew scriptures. Some of these passages will be lifted up presently as we look more closely at the relationship of eucharist to justice. Suffice it here simply to mention the Magnificat in Luke 1:46–55 ("God has brought down the powerful from their thrones, and lifted up the lowly...") and Jesus' message drawn from the prophet Isaiah in the synagogue at Nazareth (Luke 4:16–19: "The Spirit of the Lord is upon me, because he has anointed me to bring good news to the poor. He has sent me to proclaim release to the captives and recovery of sight to the blind, to let the oppressed go free, to proclaim the year of the Lord's favor"). Be sure to read the response to Jesus' message in vv. 28–30, an integral part of the text frequently and conveniently omitted in public readings.

All of these scriptures point to God as the source of justice. God's covenant with Israel in the Hebrew bible is rooted in God's righteousness and justice, which are signs of God's holiness and steadfast love. Justice upholds the rights of every person in the community.

As Bruce Birch writes in *Let Justice Roll Down*, God's justice is particularly expressed in care for the poor, the hungry, the widow, the orphan, the oppressed, the troubled, and the afflicted. Their rights are upheld by God's advocacy as basic to God's covenant with Israel. Therefore, Israel's covenant relationship with God requires the effort to embody justice in social structures and practices. This effort calls for discernment beyond merely performing the letter of the law.

For Christians Jesus personifies the continuation of God's justice-oriented covenant. Certainly not everything in the New Testament can, should, or needs to be squeezed into the theme of justice. Jesus often speaks of forgiveness, prayer, guilt, anxiety, death, acceptance, and other faith matters of a universal yet personal nature. Justice as God's will and demand is not the only way we come to know God, but if we can trust the scripture's witness, we are unlikely to know God at the deepest level apart from the reality of justice's gift and demand. Woe to those who neglect justice, Jesus tells us. When we have loosed the bonds of injustice, Isaiah tells us, *then* "your healing shall spring up quickly…your ancient ruins shall be rebuilt; you shall raise up the foundations of many generations; you shall be called the repairer of the breach, the restorer of streets to live in" (Isaiah 58:8, 12).

The Signs of Justice

The source of justice is God, according to various biblical texts in both the Hebrew Bible and Christian scriptures. What, then, are some of the signs of justice? What does justice look like? Who are those without justice? In order to do complete "justice to Justice," we would need to examine in detail the historical and literary context of each text and most likely enter into a word study of Hebrew and Greek.

Even without doing this I believe we can draw a faithful overall picture of biblical justice and justice today informed by biblical insights and imperatives. Signs of justice are these: better quality of life, equal rights and privileges, policies and procedures in the public interest or for the common good, protection of rights, more equitable sharing of resources. We see the surfacing of these concerns, as already suggested, in

Deuteronomic law, the prophets of social justice, the Psalms, and the basic orientation of Jesus' ministry. Nor, as we shall see, are these matters missing in the various New Testament epistles.

Justice is God's prescription for the well-being of a community. The so-called *Pax Romana*—the peace of Rome—was constructed on a vast system of domination and denial of justice. It collapsed by the weight of its own internal oppressions. Injustice is the kiss of death for any society. The absence of respect for any group of people, growing disparity of resources between rich and poor, systemic racism and sexism with double standards of social, economic, and political rights is a one-way street to chaos, violence, and disintegration.

Justice places special concern for the relatively powerless, marginalized, oppressed people in a given society. Who comes to mind in the United States? To use biblical images, who are the widows and orphans and sojourners in our society? Who are the outcasts and dispossessed? Who are "justice denied" people? Here are at least some of whom I see: Children. Refugees and migrant workers. The poor. Persons with disabilities. People of color. Women. Gays and lesbians. Should others be added? Persons in prison? The aging? Religious and cultural minorities? The unborn? In Chapters 5 and 6, I will address some justice implications of the eucharist in relation to several of these groups, both in the church and in society at large.

One brief way of describing justice might be this: securing the well-being and dignity of every member of the community, with concern for the common good and for the creation itself. Today most of our church bodies at least have statements supporting and encouraging an array of justice issues and concerns. In my tradition the United Methodist Social Principles, using a variety of headings, offer a supportive naming and outline of many forms of overlapping justice: economic and distributive, political and procedural, ecological, and international. In the United Methodist Social

Principles justice issues are of course connected with those of local, national, and world peace.

The movement of this chapter through the source and the signs of justice has sought to lay the groundwork for the chapter's particular claim. The eucharist as deeply public and prophetic, that is, by its very nature a sacrament of justice, now becomes a crucial focus.

Justice and Eucharist in the New Testament

1. The Pauline Corinthian Tradition

Paul's first letter to the church at Corinth provides the earliest eucharistic account in the New Testament. The Lord's supper remained an actual meal at this early date. Paul condemns the practice by which some proceed with their own meal while others go hungry. Apparently, the more affluent members arrived first with ample provisions. Working class members were not able to come until later, at which time the food was mostly consumed. The poor were virtually excluded from table fellowship. Even worse, some apparently became drunk on the wine. In these verses of 11:20–34 Paul makes it clear that the Lord's supper is a corporate act of sharing and solidarity, not an individual act of piety or self-gratification without regard to other members of the faith community.

Equal sharing when all are present, waiting for each other, and concern for those who have nothing implies equality, a foundation for Justice. Justice within the church is a necessity for internal cohesion and for the church's witness beyond the church. The faithfulness and integrity of the church's witness to the world cannot be separated from the church's internal relationships. Participating in the meal without consideration of others is an insult to Christ, the host. The manner in which the meal is celebrated is itself a witness to justice or injustice.

2. The Synoptic-Passover Tradition

The three gospels of Matthew, Mark, and Luke treat the preparation of the Lord's supper as a Passover meal. At the very least we can say the meal is closely connected with the Passover tradition in the eyes of the early church, though there are variations within the three gospels regarding both the sequence and the wording surrounding the bread and the cup.

Matthew and Mark follow a closely related pattern. During the meal Jesus takes a loaf of bread, blesses it, breaks it, and gives it to his disciples. This fourfold action characterizes the feeding of the multitudes in Mark 6 and 8, as well as the Emmaus story in Luke 24. The disciples take and eat and are told by Jesus, "This is my body." Then Jesus takes the cup, gives thanks, and gives it to the disciples. In Matthew's account, Jesus says, "Drink from it, all of you; for this is my blood of the covenant, which is poured out for many for the forgiveness of sins" (26:27–28). In Mark, Jesus says, "This is my blood of the covenant, which is poured out for many" (14:24). According to the NRSV, other ancient authors add *new* in front of the word covenant.

Luke provides a quite different order and wording of the Lord's supper. Here Jesus takes and gives the cup before taking the loaf of bread. Then he passes the cup again after supper, saying it is poured out as the new covenant in his blood. Perhaps most surprising, it is only in Luke of the synoptic gospels that Jesus is portrayed as saying, "Do this in remembrance of me" (22:19), referring to the bread and presumably the cup as well.

The meal in the upper room shared by Jesus and his disciples obviously has many parallels to the Jewish Passover meal. The blessing and sharing of bread and wine is rooted in the Jewish *berakah*, a prayer of blessing and thanksgiving to God. The sacrificial sense of Jesus' words regarding his body and blood are seen by his disciples as a reference to the Passover Lamb sacrificed in the Jewish Passover. As the Jewish Passover remembers the liberation of the Hebrews from slavery under Pharaoh, so the Supper of the Lord is to be remembered as a meal of liberation from bondage through the self-giving of Jesus Christ.

For Christians the essential point is this: We remember (*anamnesis*) not only a historical event in the upper room, but the One to be remembered through the act of bread and cup. We don't "do the eucharist" just to follow a command in numbing ritualistic obedience. The eucharist is a concrete, focused event by which we are to be formed in the image of Jesus Christ. To partake of the communion elements "in remembrance of me" is to remember the barrier breaker–community maker, the champion of the poor, the Prince of Peace, the defender of justice in the long tradition of the prophets of Israel. It is *this* Lord whom we are called to feed upon, to receive as our exemplar, and to emulate in word and deed through the empowerment of God's grace.

The Christian Passover, or Lord's supper, is more than a call to justice, but it cannot be less. After all, we don't remember just anyone. We remember a specific person through a specific event. "Do this" is not only a call to a ritual act but also a call to do the life of Jesus Christ, or in other terms, to walk the talk. "What we have in the eucharist is a community gathering at God's behest to embody the character of God. In this community Messiah Jesus as the host personifies the mystery of God righting our human condition at its deepest level" (Herzog 1988, 132).

I have been asked more than once, "Are persons who are clearly not committed to justice welcome at the welcome table if they are baptized Christians?" One can imagine varying contexts applicable to this question. I believe an appropriate direction is suggested in the following account:

> Once I was in a small village in Latin America where the *hacienda* owner asked to take part in the eucharists of the peasants' basic Christian community. He was welcomed with the reminder that if he chose to share the broken bread that the peasants had managed to retain from their exploited sweat, his sharing in their labors could not stop at that point. (Power, *Worship* 1985, 451)

3. The Emmaus Tradition: From Last Supper to Everlasting Supper

The upper room tradition of the synoptic gospels focuses on the sacrifice or self-giving of Christ. A somber foretaste of death is in the air, a pre-resurrection event. But the supper of the Lord does not end there.

Most Christians are also familiar with another account of Jesus breaking bread with his followers in Luke 24:13–35. Now we're on the road to the village of Emmaus. Mary Magdalene, Joanna, Mary the mother of James, and other women with them have already announced the resurrection to the eleven male apostles. The women were the first evangelists of the resurrection. The male followers were the first unbelievers, scoffing at the women's story.

So Jesus, unrecognized, joins Cleopas and his companion along the road. Lengthy conversation follows concerning Jesus' death. Jesus chides them for not believing the women and the prophets concerning the resurrection. As the day is late, they urge him to stay with them. At the table we read of familiar action: He takes the bread, blesses and breaks it, and gives it to them. In the breaking of bread they recognize the risen Christ. They exclaim in wonder how he opened the scriptures to them while they were on the road. They return to Jerusalem to tell the eleven what has happened to them on the road and how he was known to them in the breaking of the bread.

As I suggested in chapter 3, in the Emmaus tradition the Last Supper has become the Everlasting Supper. The truth of the Christ of love and justice cannot be destroyed. The dominant image of the eucharist becomes one of triumphant joy and celebration rather than one of seemingly impending defeat. The two events inform and transform each other as a single continuum. If the Lord's supper in the upper room had been the Last Supper, it would have died out in the first generation of Christians or else become a morbid memorial. But there can be no resurrection that has not passed through death. So we have a feast with Christ, the vulnerable-victorious Host.

> We do well to be wary of a chirpy over-reaction that fastens onto the joy of resurrection and fails to see that no one can rise from the dead except by first dying. Nothing is gained if we replace one distortion with another. So we do well to follow carefully the lead of the Synoptic Gospels as they join death and resurrection in an indissoluble bond. Anything less is either too good to be true or too desolate to be endured in the name of the Gospel. (Stookey 1993, 37)

As Christians we can consider the eucharist as an everlasting supper, a living enactment of the reign of God personified in Jesus. As such the eucharist holds before us a vision of a world made whole and a people united in peace, justice, and love. The eucharist points to the renewal of the social order where there is enough to eat for everyone, where all stand or kneel on the equal ground of divine grace and thus the ground of worth and dignity.

The Testimony of Latin American Christians

The church in the United States can come to a deeper experience of the eucharist by learning from Latin American Christians. In some Latin American churches the meal is more likely to be experienced as a joyous celebrative feast with the Lord, a liberating sacrament calling forth justice and dignity in societal structures.

It was no accident that Salvadoran Archbishop Romero was assassinated (1980) while celebrating the eucharist. Nor was it by chance that in several villages the Salvadoran military destroyed the altar and all visible reminders of the eucharist. The powers and principalities were theologically bankrupt but not theologically naive. It was no secret that for many Salvadoran Christians the eucharist as a meal of liberation reflected the Reign of God and, thus, a transformed society. Eucharistic celebrations with great joy and hope by the poor are definitely not welcome in some places.

The Testimony of Eucharistic Liturgies and Prayers

Since the Second Vatican Council both Roman Catholic and Protestant scholars have paid more attention to the liturgies of the early church. Protestant leaders in particular have come to make more conscious use of the fourfold eucharistic action of taking, blessing, breaking, and giving the bread. As we have seen, this action from the upper room and the Emmaus event arise from the Jewish table blessing.

The Great Thanksgiving can claim to be a basic form of Christian worship in much of Christian history. Here I want to point to one example from a typical prayer of Great Thanksgiving which suggests the Justice orientation of the eucharist:

> Holy are you and blessed is your son Jesus Christ.
> Your Spirit anointed him
> to preach good news to the poor,
> to proclaim release to the captives
> and recovering sight to the blind,
> to set at liberty those who are oppressed,
> and to announce that the time had come
> when you would save your people. (*UMH* 1985, 9)

These words come from Luke 4 by way of Isaiah 61. Many prayers of thanksgiving include references to exodus, such as "you delivered us from captivity." The Lord's Prayer, frequently prayed before the breaking and sharing of bread, explicitly beseeches God's reign now.

The Testimony of Bread and Wine: From God and Back to God

In one way or another most Christians believe in the presence of Christ in the eucharistic bread and wine, or at least in the total community action of the sacrament. The conviction that Christ is present in bread and cup can offer an expanded view of the eucharist, especially its public and prophetic dimension.

What goes into making a loaf of bread and a cup of wine? In *Spirituality and Liberation* Robert McAfee Brown offers a reply:

> The bread and wine are available only because there has
> been planting, cultivating, harvesting, gathering, ferment-
> ing or baking, storing, transporting, distributing, buying,
> and selling—in short, all those things we identify with the
> life of economics and politics. (Brown 1988, 92)

In other words all the stuff of our common life is wrapped
up in the elements of bread and wine.

These are the gifts of God for which we have
responsibility to offer back to God. They represent all the
gifts and efforts of human labor made possible by God. They
represent a trust from God to be returned through systems
of justice. When I see the common loaf and the chalice on the
table or altar, I see much more than an invitation to strengthen
my personal spirituality, as essential as that is for me and for
others. I see covenant, community, and connections. I see the
world of commerce and international trade and labor
practices, meant to be under the dominion of the God of
justice.

There is more to see in the bread and the chalice. My
friend Ruben Habito has helped me to ask similar questions
from an ecological standpoint. Once again, what goes into
making a loaf of bread and a cup of wine? Rain. Sunshine.
Wind. Photosynthesis. Soil. All of the interaction of God's
creation. Independent of human labor yet dependent on God-
given human labor for turning wheat and grape into bread
and wine.

When I see the bread and the cup, I see the totality of
God's gifts to us and our calling to offer these gifts back to
God in a way that praises God and promotes human liberation. I see the wonder and beauty of the created order, the
sheer gift of God apart from human effort. I see the interaction of God and humanity for partnership in shaping the
ongoing life of the world. I can weep at what the human race
has done to the earth and to each other. I can rejoice at the
mystery and magnificence of God's goodness and the God-
given capacity of human love and goodwill. Credit a simple
loaf of bread and a humble cup of wine.

We have it on good authority that God chose what is foolish in the world to shame the wise; what is weak in the world to shame the strong; what is low and despised in the world to bring to nothing things that are, or as the NEB says it, "to overthrow the existing order" (from 1 Corinthians 1).

Justice, Not Just Us

God as the source of justice; some signs of justice; testimonies to a sacrament of justice—this is the terrain we've been traversing in this chapter. Now I raise two questions for consideration. The first one, asked in several ways, is this: Is a sacrament which is profoundly public and prophetic a promise or a threat? Is justice good news or bad news? Is a meal of liberation a heritage to be welcomed or one to be held in suspicion?

Many Christians are committed in word and deed to a just society. There is a realization that injustices, whether economic, political, or social, spawn a dysfunctional society of instability and alienation. Positively said, a just society encourages goodwill, reconciliation, and policies and procedures promoting the well-being of all citizens. My sense is that many Christians also realize that while most issues of justice can be complex and ambiguous, commitment to the lordship of Jesus Christ is a commitment requiring willingness to work with these issues.

Commitment to justice can be costly in a number of ways. Least of all is the cost of time, although justice is hard and time-consuming work. A society's ethos of injustice has usually accumulated over a period of years like stubborn barnacles on a ship. Very seldom does entrenched power give up privilege willingly or swiftly. Most costly of all is the potential risk of personal and family threats received. Civil rights and anti-war positions can draw heavy flak. Martyrdom need not be sought, but should the cross be no more than sanctuary furniture or around-the-neck decoration?

Justice requires Christians to abandon the "just us" mentality. Martin Luther King, Jr. reminded us that we are all "in an inescapable network of mutuality, tied together in a single garment of destiny" (King 1963, 70). Some years ago Orbis Books published my book, *Good News is Bad News, is Good News*. My premise was—and remains—that the Good News of the gospel may sound like bad news until we come to be where the gospel calls us to be. It has long been said that Good News for the poor is of course bad news for the rich. Precisely so. However, there is more to say. I like to use the Exodus drama featuring God, Moses and Aaron, Pharaoh, and the Hebrew people as a test case. "Let my people go" had to be the worst news possible for Pharaoh. His entire oppressive political and economic system was doomed. Bad news indeed.

But what if Pharaoh had heeded God's word? He didn't, but what if he had done so? The Good News that was his bad news would become his profoundest and only hope, indeed the best news he could possibly hear. He was offered release from destroying the lives of others as well as his own. The Good News that came as bad news could become his good news: "Let my people go and receive from me a new life."

In the final analysis there can be only one Good News, although it requires very different responses from different people and groups according to their life circumstances. Anyone who has ever been part of family intervention with a chemically dependent member knows that the intended good news of sobriety is likely to be received initially as bad news with resistance and denial. Only acceptance with hard work over a period of time reveals the message of life-saving good news.

I learned a long time ago that God loves me enough to disturb me. This is likely to be painful at the time but efficacious later. The demands of justice ask us to give up some privileges, to change some ways of thinking, to see that people are more important than things. But in justice there is life—the life of God who creates community and welcomes us in love.

Is justice a threat or a promise? Both! I like to place the gift and the challenge in the following context:

If you in this country keep working in whatever ways you can for the crucified people of the earth—in the United States, in El Salvador, wherever—your lives will have more meaning; your faith will be more Christian; your hope will be stronger. (Sobrino 1989)

The second question in this closing section is this: If the church is to be about the task of justice, how might it do so? What would the task look like?

"The Liturgical assembly will not provide a model of perfection or easy answers to social justice issues. But it will hold up a vision of what might be" (Henderson 1989, 20). These words remind us that the eucharist will not offer simple solutions but will raise profound questions with some theological contours and clues for the church's social justice concerns and actions. Hopefully mutually supportive sermon and sacrament can serve as a unified double agent on behalf of stimulating justice thought and action.

The church functions on many levels. National. Regional. Local. Ecumenical. Small task groups. Justice at work has many faces according to specific contexts. Here are a few examples I know about:

> Examining power and roles within the local and denominational church as a means of practicing and witnessing justice.

> Addressing city councils and school boards regarding policies perceived to be discriminatory towards people of color, females, gays and lesbians, or economically impoverished neighborhoods.

> Ecumenically improving plans for summer reading programs and food distribution for children in various areas of the metroplex with the aim of complementing an inadequate system of public assistance.

> Taking advocacy stances on behalf of children before county and state legislatures.

Encouraging programs which support economic development in low-income areas and availability of low-cost housing.

Supporting policies and procedures in churches and in all public buildings to provide access for developmentally disabled persons.

Becoming informed on U.S. immigration law and calling for just and humane immigration laws and practice.

Calling for a just criminal justice system, that is, a system that does not discriminate against the poor and people of color.

These examples sound somewhat generic, but they are all taken from actual attempts to serve the cause of justice. Virtually all of them arose from contact with people on the short end of justice and were developed where possible through a cooperative effort with persons whose lives were affected. In every situation a considerable amount of homework and fact-finding was involved over a period of time.

Can you add your own examples to those suggested here?

We turn now to how participation in the eucharist can lead to advocacy by the church for inclusivity and justice with specific groups of people.

5

Living the Eucharist in Today's World (A)

We must break out of the circle of self-absorption
and pay heed to the bloodied face of our fellow human
beings. For they are the great sacrament of God, the signs
and instruments of authentic divine reality. If we do not
share life with the oppressed, we do not share life with God.
(Boff 1980, 48)

Who was Jesus? The church has a long list of descriptions: Messiah, Lord, Christ, Redeemer, Master, Savior, Son of God. There are other descriptions as well: Jew; refugee; advocate for children, women, outcasts, and the poor; friend of sinners, sufferers, and Samaritans. These latter descriptions tell us much about our identity and imperatives as Christians. They also tell us much about the state of the church, its past history, and our present and future opportunities.

When we take Jesus into ourselves at his invitation in the eucharist, we are under orders to live eucharistically toward all of our neighbors. What difference does participation in the eucharist make for Christians in relation to all those whom Jesus befriended and for whom he lived and died? How might the eucharist shape Christian theology and practice in relation to Jews in a post-Holocaust history?

This chapter will not pretend to offer a substantive analysis of these questions. They are much too deep and complex to approach in simplistic or abbreviated manner. What I do intend is an inquiry encouraging *awareness* of the eucharist's bearing on these questions. A few clues can be offered for living out the love and justice already given at the welcome table and far beyond.

The eucharist, is of course, one way among many of relating the Christian gospel to the people and issues chosen for this chapter and the next. I hope you will find some fresh connections here between the eucharist and what Christians are called to be about in the world.

Living the Eucharist after the Experience of the Shoah

Shoah is a Hebrew term for the Holocaust during the time of Hitler's regime of horror throughout Europe. Shoah is generally used to refer to the six million Jews who perished as a result of Hitler's "final solution." Sometimes Shoah may refer to the eleven million persons who lost their lives, thus including five million non-Jews. Jewish and Christian theologians and philosophers continue to struggle with how to theologize in response to the Shoah. The term post-Shoah theology is used to designate the bewildering task of theological reflection and dialogue following the demise of Hitler and Nazi Germany in 1945.

The Shoah is, of course, one context among many by which Christians may consider Jewish-Christian relations. The Shoah as exclusive context may lead Christians to view Jews strictly as victims rather than as a people who have greatly enriched history in countless ways. Even so, I have chosen here the experience of the Shoah as a significant influence on Christian thinking and practice. After all, the primary response of the church to the Holocaust, or more correctly, the lack of response, was and remains the antithesis of eucharistic meaning.

A Shoah or post-Shoah theology for Christians necessitates a vast overhaul of the way much Christian theology has been done throughout Christian history. The pre-Shoah theology we Christians have inherited has often communicated more contempt than respect for Jewish thought and practice, even when we have not intended to do so. Awareness that this is so is the first positive step Christians can take in addressing this deplorable situation. Even a cursory historical knowledge of pogroms and other acts of persecution perpetrated by Christians against Jews should be more than ample evidence to suggest a major reconstruction of Christian teaching.

Our most instructive teacher can be the record of the Christian church during the Holocaust or Shoah. The complicity of Christian teaching and practice in contributing to the Holocaust is well documented. Mordecai Paldiel reminds us in his book *Sheltering the Jews*:

> The churches themselves had paradoxically paved the way for Hitler's ruthless treatment of the Jews. For generations, church teachings derided the Jews as a perverse and culpable people who lived under God's wrath for not accepting the Christian faith. (Paldiel 1996, 30)

Leading churchmen cultivated the deicide charge in the minds of many Christians. Paldiel continues:

> In Germany, most evangelical church pastors swore fidelity to Hitler in 1938 and adopted the Aryan clause in their churches, directed at Jewish converts to Christianity. In flagrant disregard of Christian teachings, "non-Aryan" Christians were either removed or fully segregated in their churches. In a 1941 statement, several church leaders in Germany publicly consented to have abolished all fellowship with Jewish Christians. (Paldiel 1996, 31)
>
> In light of the traditional theological anti-Semitism, coupled with the silence of church hierarchies at the Nazi anti-Jewish measures, it is indeed miraculous that

not a few of the clergy extended help to Jews in various ways. Those offering assistance were to be found in significant numbers in both Catholic and Protestant churches, more so in Western Europe, and relatively less in Eastern Europe. (Paldiel 1996, 33)

The response of the church beyond Germany during the Shoah is also dismal.

The great democracies maintained their stiff pre-war quota systems, which allowed no more than a trickle of Jews to be admitted to their countries (witness the *Saint Louis* affair, where a boatload of more than nine hundred German Jews was refused landing on Cuban and U.S. shores and made to sail back to Europe). (Paldiel 1996, 6–7)

Christian readers of this book are not likely to be responsible for the Holocaust. We *are* responsible today, however, for the way we theologize and live out Christian faith in relation to Judaism. We do have the opportunity to espouse a faith which encourages respect and appreciation for our Jewish sisters and brothers and Jewish faith. All too often Christian teaching has embraced these positions: Jews have been interpreted as Christ killers (deicide); Christianity is proclaimed as superior, Judaism as inferior; God's covenant with Israel is seen as being canceled and replaced with the covenant in Jesus Christ; Jews are said to be condemned because they do not accept Jesus as the Messiah; some New Testament texts are used to justify anti-Semitism; Christianity is held forth as characterized by grace and spirituality, Judaism as legalistic and bound by law and works righteousness.

Living the eucharist after the Shoah, on the other hand, would encourage the following, a direction in Christian thought by no means unknown and yet in need of broadening and deepening.

- The God Christians are called to glorify and in whom we live, and move, and have our being is the God of Israel.

- The embodiment of God in Christian eyes was in the form of Jewish flesh.

- The covenant of God with Israel and the covenant of God through Jesus Christ stand side by side to love God and neighbor as articulated in each covenant.

- Jewish brothers and sisters are Christians' elder brothers and sisters from whom we learned God's gifts of word and table from synagogue and Jewish family Sabbath meal.

- Jesus continued the great prophetic tradition of the Hebrew prophets which claims the allegiance of Jews and Christians alike.

- Christian credibility in the world lies not in claims of superiority to other faiths—not in triumphalism and imperious claims—but in love and justice for neighbor and creation.

- Jesus' proclamation and embodiment of the Kingdom or Rule of God was a threat, and yet a promise, to both the political and religious establishment of his time and of every age and culture.

- For Christians Jesus' death is a sign of the human condition especially related to power and pride in all human communities; a sign of faithfulness to his vocation of justice and love; a seal of solidarity with the oppressed of all nations and cultures; and a call to the church and to individual Christians for a life of self-giving freely and intentionally chosen on behalf of others.

- The church could designate one day as Yom HaShoah, "Holocaust Day," as does the Jewish calendar, thus observing an appropriate corporate memory and a dedication toward those tasks which Holocaust memory demands.

As Christians we have an immense agenda of rethinking our doctrines and how they are articulated. Every Christian has control over his or her own expression of Christian belief. A good place to work on one's beliefs is in dialogue with Jewish brothers and sisters, with strong listening emphasis on the Christian's part.

In *Sheltering the Jews* Mordecai Paldiel relates the stories of Holocaust rescuers and those whom they rescued. These brave rescuers have been accorded the title "Righteous among the Nations." Their names are recorded at Yad VaShem, the Holocaust Memorial in Jerusalem commemorating the six million Jewish victims who perished at the hands of the Nazis and their collaborators.

One story of martyrdom recounts the heroism of Elizaveta Skobtzova, better known as Mère Marie of the Russian Orthodox Church branch in Paris:

> Together with her assistant, Father Dimitri Klepinin, she transformed the church's facility in Paris into a refuge for Jews. Disregarding threats to their personal safety, both were eventually arrested by the Gestapo in March 1943 and deported to Dora and Ravensbrück camps, where they perished. Among her personal notes, the following words give testimony to the woman's altruistic fervor: "At the Last Judgment, I will not be asked whether I satisfactorily practiced asceticism, or how many bows I have made before the divine altar. I will be asked whether I fed the hungry, clothed the naked, visited the sick and prisoner in his jail. That is all that will be asked. (Paldiel 1996, 42–43)

Would you and I have responded differently than did most German Christians, as well as Christians of some of the other European countries? Would we have had the courage to shelter Jews? If we were adults at the time of the Holocaust, did we speak out in this country on behalf of the Jews in Europe? Each of us can ponder these questions in dialogue with our own soul. Perhaps it is impossible to know for sure. What is possible, indeed necessary, is for each of us as Christians to be aware of how Christian thought and practice can reveal either contempt or respect for Judaism and our Jewish brothers and sisters...and to be aware of the possible consequences.

To be partakers of the body and blood of Jesus Christ in the sacrament is to care for the bodies and blood of our Jewish neighbors as though they were our own. The sacrament of Christ's body and blood should awaken and empower Christians to recognize the sacramental presence of our colleagues in God's covenantal love. Eucharist without moral imperative is the shameful practice of cheap grace. When Christians disregard the worth, the dignity, and the rights of Jews, we deny Christ himself.

Spreading the Welcome Table with Children

Do we think of hungry children when we participate in the eucharist? Not every time, I'm sure, but now and again? "The body of Christ for you" surely cannot be disconnected from the malnourished bodies of millions of children. Would Jesus, the host of the meal, be unconcerned for hungry children?

Familiar words help us to make the connection: "Let the little children come to me; do not stop them; for it is to such as these that the kingdom of God belongs. Truly I tell you, whoever does not receive the kingdom of God as a little child will never enter it." These words of Jesus in the Gospel of Mark are followed by "he took them up in his arms, laid his hands on them, and blessed them" (Mark 10:13–16). The same story is told in Matthew 19:13–15 and Luke 18:15–17. In Matthew 18 Jesus tells his disciples, "Whoever welcomes one such child in my name welcomes me" (v. 5), an assertion also made in Mark 9 and Luke 9.

In Mark 5 Jesus is implored by Jairus, a synagogue leader, to heal his daughter, who is at the point of death. When Jesus arrives at Jairus' house he gathers the girl's father and mother and those who were with him at the girl's bedside. He takes her by the hand and bids her to arise. Life is restored. Jesus' departing words are for those present to give her something to eat (Mark 5:35–43). The story's ending is reminiscent of the feeding story of the five thousand in the next chapter. The disciples want to send the crowd away, but Jesus tells his disciples, "You give them something to eat." The disciples do not understand, and Jesus feeds the crowd by spreading the table for everyone.

Can we spread the Lord's welcome table beyond the sanctuary into the lives of children in poverty? Are we giving them something to eat, something in which to hope? Statistics are cold by themselves and can be overwhelming to the point that we throw up our hands in despair, guilt, or denial. For instance, there are at least 25 million refugees, globally speaking, displaced from their homes and living on the edge of hopelessness. Two-thirds are children.

The Children's Defense Fund literature and other sources say that approximately one out of five children in the United States lives in poverty. One out of every two black children and two out of five Hispanic children live in poverty. (West 1993, 7). That's about 16 million—and 9 million are without health care. In his book *The Eucharist and Human Liberation*, Tissa Balasuriya says of several areas in Sri Lanka (formerly Ceylon), "Here tens of thousands live in terrible squalor and misery in the shadow of monumental churches. Over one hundred thousand masses have been celebrated in these places over the decades" (Balasuriya 1979, xii). Is there no connection? Shouldn't there be?

Statistics don't bleed, but children do. The systemic violence of poverty stacks the deck and stalks the life of many if not most of its survivors for a lifetime in terms of mental and emotional and physical health, educational advancement, job opportunity, and self-image—unless, of course, there is intervention on the part of the religious community and other concerned citizens, and a network of public support. If so-called welfare reform reduces what has been available for women, infants, and children in terms of nutrition, healthcare, Headstart, and foster care, leaving children worse off rather than better, we will have a further deforming of our society rather than a reforming.

The eucharist will not tell us specifically what to do in relation to hungry and abused children. But it can convey a grace calling forth awareness and responsibility. It can motivate us to search for those ways in which we can make a difference, even a small one, surely a more promising prospect than making no difference at all. Maybe individually, maybe through a task group, maybe in concert with other churches. The risen Christ of the Everlasting Supper invites, even commands, us to spread the welcome table of hospitality, compassion, and justice to children far and wide. In his book *God-Walk*, the late Frederick Herzog reminds us that we practice "closed communion" if the hunger of the world is disassociated with the bread and wine of the eucharist (Herzog 1988, 130–41).

Sometimes spreading that table will take the form of compassion, sometimes of justice advocacy. The church can educate its members about the needs of children and the poor, make church facilities safe and welcoming, involve children in the life of the church, and support legislation and public policies that improve children's lives and lives of poor families. One thing is certain. To spread the table worldwide for children is not just for their well-being, but for ours as well.

Here is one example of spreading the welcome table to children in an urban area. As we shall see in the next chapter, no congregation is too small to make a difference. Sometimes, however, the cooperation of many churches can help to accomplish what a single congregation would find impossible.

The Greater Dallas Community of Churches, composed of over 300 congregations, assists in coordinating and, where possible, expanding a Summer Food Program offering free meals to children ages one to eighteen in low-income neighborhoods. As many as 25–30 thousand children at more than 200 locations throughout the Dallas metroplex benefit from the program.

The Community of Churches works with local school districts, nonprofit groups, city government, corporations, and foundations to maintain the program in the face of cuts in welfare funding to the Summer Food Program. Present legislative changes reduced federal reimbursements that school districts or city government collect for operating food programs. Without the program the children, who receive free lunches during the school year, would have inadequate summertime nutrition. The Community of Churches identifies new sites and recruits volunteers to provide enrichment and recreational activities.

A summer reading program at eighteen sites is also provided by Community of Churches volunteers. About two thousand children will develop their reading skills by reading thirty minutes a day to a caring volunteer. The adult and teen volunteers spend two hours a day listening to and talking with the children as they develop confidence in reading. The children draw pictures, act out the story line, and answer questions related to the reading. Two out of three third-graders in the neediest neighborhoods read below grade level. Improvement in reading can improve self-esteem, the likelihood of staying in school, and sound life choices (Stoesz 1997).

When you partake of Christ's body and blood, remember the body and blood of children.

Spreading the Welcome Table with the Poor

You are aware by now, if I have written clearly, that I use the term "spreading the welcome table" to mean extending God's love and justice, reflected in the eucharist, into the world, with special concern for particular histories and groups of people. Another way to explain the term is through a question: What does it mean for Christians to live eucharistically in the world in a way that reflects the mind and example of Christ?

Spreading the welcome table also has a second meaning, namely, inclusivity. The hymn for which this book is named states, "Here all the world will find a welcome." Our Jewish brothers and sisters celebrate the holy meal of the Sabbath and the Passover, a testimony to God's liberating action and call to the covenant of love and justice. Christians should respect the Jewish holy meal as we do the eucharist and rejoice in these two mutually supportive covenants. The Christian eucharist is spread to children, the poor, and the other groups to be mentioned in this chapter and the next as partakers around an inclusive table.

The Christian eucharist welcomed the rich and the poor in the Corinthian church and should do so in every generation. God knows even when we don't that we need each other in order to have true community. Spreading the welcome table with the poor, however, means more than a worship service in which both rich and poor are welcome to participate in the eucharist.

Communion is more than bread and chalice shared in corporate worship. Communion is a way of life in which bread and goods are shared. Spreading the table of sharing provides a perspective on the conditions of people in the world and what it means to be a true neighbor. Christians in the early centuries were hardly unaware of the eucharistic implications.

Listen in your mind to Saint John Chrysostom, fourth-century ecumenical Patriarch of Constantinople:

> "He who said, 'This is my Body' is the same who said, 'You saw me, a hungry man, and you did not give me to eat.' Of what use is it to load the table of Christ? Feed the hungry and then come and decorate the table. You are making a golden chalice and you do not give a cup of cold water? The temple of your afflicted brother's body is more precious than this Temple (the church). The Body of Christ becomes for you an altar. It is more holy than the altar of stone on which you celebrate the holy sacrifice. You are able to contemplate this altar everywhere, in the street and in open squares." (Balasuriya 1979, 26–27)

If the church makes no connection between the eucharist and the poor, the church prostitutes the meal and risks becoming a Society for the Protection and Preservation of the Privileged and the Prosperous instead of a friend and advocate of the poor. Instead of spreading the table of Christ we turn it into a privileged meal, which anesthetizes us against the world's injustices. Would even Christ the host be welcome?

A twenty-seven member congregation in north Texas is providing food for 465 families per week. Church volunteers participate in a church-based ministry that distributes perishable food to people in four counties from grocery shelves in the Dallas area. Every Saturday morning pickup trucks with fruits, vegetables, and other perishable foods back up to the door of the church. Fruits and vegetables are placed in separate rooms, and bread and cakes are spread across the back of the sanctuary on a large table and stacked on the back of pews.

Some families come to the church to pick up the food they need. Home deliveries are made. Arrangements are also made for direct delivery to a church in another city where people can obtain needed food. Some food is used by Meals on Wheels in a nearby town. The ministry continues to expand on Wednesdays and Fridays, and volunteers from several denominations are involved. "We feed anybody who's hungry," says one volunteer.

So the volunteers of a twenty-seven-member church help feed more families over a four-county area in north Texas in a week than will attend worship at the church in six months. They call it "Loaves of Love" (Robertson, 1997).

The Lord's table of hospitality is spread beyond the sanctuary into the lives of families in need. In my mind, this is the eucharist on the move, where Christ as host is indeed made visible where it counts the most. In the Kingdom or Rule of God, justice will prevail and there will be sufficient food for every child, woman, and man. In the meantime, even as we work for just systems, Christ's followers are to be spreading the table far and wide as a sign of God's presence and unconditional love.

This eucharistic life of service, risk, and responsibility is sustained by the eucharist itself. For most of us it is tempting to hide and easy to evade. We can be obsessed with guilt and failure. Caring can bring fatigue and discouragement. In the final analysis the eucharist is centered not in our human condition—either success or failure—but in God's irrepressible, unconditional, everlasting love. The Everlasting Supper is meant to be an experience of joyful discernment, discovery, and disclosure rooted in the vulnerable, victorious Lord, just as it was in the village of Emmaus in Jesus' breaking of the bread.

Eucharistic life does not promise ease, success, or glory in terms of the world. It does not guarantee emotional or physical health, even if there are many who in fact *are* healthier due to their faith. Eucharistic life offers the recurring possibility of giving and receiving in the way of Christ and thus participating in the life of God. Eucharistic life is when "you decide to live for a truth in which the only assurance of victory is the victory of living for that truth" (McElvaney 1971, 99).

Spreading the Welcome Table with Refugees

The stories heard firsthand leave an indelible imprint on the mind and heart: A family member disappearing at the hands of death squads. Constant threats of torture. A wife raped, a husband forced into servitude. A whole village massacred. Starving children. Nocturnal escape. Walking unbelievable distance under the direst of circumstances. Returning from refugee camps to destroyed homes. Can most of us even imagine it?

First were the Salvadorans, a few Nicaraguans, and Hondurans. Then the Guatemalans. More recently, Somalis, Kenyans, Nigerians. From more than thirty countries they come, compelled by hope, driven by fear, desiring a decent life of basic family values, looking for work, for adequate food and housing. Who among us would not seek a better life under the same circumstances?

For a number of years I have served in several volunteer capacities with Proyecto Adelante (Project Onward), a non-profit, tax-exempt agency in Dallas, dedicated to protecting human rights of refugees and immigrants. The organization provides immigration counseling and representation along with social services to Central Americans and other refugees who seek asylum from violence and terror in their home-lands. Proyecto Adelante provides a job bank, an immigrant domestic violence relief act project, and a center for survi-vors of torture.

My volunteer efforts, meager compared to many others, have involved board membership and providing occasional intake interviews with refugees. The latter in particular has made it possible to hear firsthand the stories of people who have fled their homelands for reasons stated above. This ex-perience has convinced me that much anti-immigrant senti-ment would evaporate or at least diminish if more people could meet immigrants in person and hear both their stories of desperation and their visions of a hopeful future. When immigration is personalized in this way, we are very likely to see the pride, the beauty, the fragility of courageous persons.

They are often called illegal aliens, wetbacks, and worse. Some we never meet because they die on the way, nameless and unnoticed. I have no desire to sentimentalize immigrants or to overlook human faults, whether in individuals or groups. But if we listen and look closely, we will likely expe-rience gifts of faith, courage, and determination. We might see images of our own immigrant ancestors and the birthing of renewed hope in thousands of brothers and sisters.

What might it mean for Christians to live eucharistically on behalf of immigrants? To spread the welcome table of Christ? A beginning place might combine the Hebrew Bible emphasis on loving the sojourner or stranger with Jesus' ex-ample of transgressing borders, as put by Fr. Virgilio

Elizondo. The eucharist recalls all those other meals shared by Jesus with outcasts and strangers. Man-made borders (they were male-controlled then and are significantly so today) were subject to the humanity given my God in the life and teaching of Jesus. God's love is borderless love, rejecting the often artificial limits imposed by society.

The fact is we cross so-called borders as a constant way of life. We cross borders when we buy goods or eat food from other countries; when we participate in international trade; when we learn languages or customs from other lands; when we enjoy films, paintings, novels, and other forms of artistic expression from other nations. Virtually all of us are borderless in a practical sense, and we are called in a theological sense to be borderless in our basic attitude and actions towards immigrants.

Most of us instantly recognize the words, "I was a stranger and you welcomed me" (or failed to do so) from Matthew 25. Words with an -*xen* stem in New Testament Greek can mean "stranger" but also "guest." Our word *xenophobia* comes from this Greek root and indicates an irrational fear of strangers or those who seem different from ourselves. Love of the *xenos* is a special form of love of neighbor. In this parable Jesus himself is the xenos, so that "in the most alien of aliens Jesus himself is loved" (Bromiley 1985, 663).

When we as the church spread the welcome table of inclusivity and justice, our individual and collective lives participate in the sacred struggle of God in history. We turn now in chapter Six to continue reflections on living the eucharist in today's world.

6

Living the Eucharist in Today's World (B)

The Kingdom of God is like a seed planted in a woman's
   heart
slowly, silently stretching it
beyond family and friends, church and nation
until one day the heart bursts open
revealing a table
wider than the world
warm as an intimate embrace.
                    (Sister M. Robinson 1985, 146)

As a reader I have an aversion to marathon chapters, even in a book I consider to be worthwhile. As an author I should go and do likewise. Thus, I have divided chapters 5 and 6 into two segments, concerned with the same issue: developing awareness of the eucharist's connection with our world and advocacy for spreading the welcome table in terms of inclusivity and justice. In this chapter, then, we continue our reflection on spreading the welcome table.

Spreading the Welcome Table with Women
"This is my body, given for you; this is my blood, the blood of life, given for you." These hallowed words of the communion service are also the words that birthing women

can say in truth to their children. In *Sunday School Manifesto*, Elizabeth Dodson Gray points out, "Breast milk is women's blood with the red blood cells removed, and it sustains life in infants and also passes on her precious antibodies" (Gray 1994, 2). Embodied self-giving comes together in these words and experiences, reminding us of the natural relationship between holy communion and women. And to think that for so many years patriarchal dominance prevented women from being the celebrants of the eucharist...and continues to do so in some traditions.

If only the church would pay more attention to Jesus Christ! In a one-dimensional patriarchal culture Jesus unfailingly relates to women as equals. Consider the low status of women in Jesus' time: In the light of victimization, double standards, lack of human rights, and perceived inferiority in worth, Jesus' regard for women stands out like a beacon in a sea of darkness. What seems more astounding is that this subversive activity on Jesus' part somehow passed inspection by or in spite of male editors and redactors and was left as we see it in the canon of the New Testament. How can one account for this? The best I can do is to attribute it to the work of the Spirit, who somehow manages at times and places to break through human arrogance and blindness.

We need to think of only a few New Testament examples that lift up the role of women in the early church. Magnificat Mary, who birthed "the uncontrollable mystery on the bestial floor" (Yeats 1958, 141), and whose deep faith in God's promise glorified God and the humanity of the poor. Martha, who provided hospitality and sustenance. Mary, who became Jesus' student. The Samaritan woman, who provided a drink to a thirsty Jesus and who had the courage to return to her city and testify, "Come and see..." The woman with a twelve-year hemorrhage, who took initiative to touch the fringe of Jesus' cloak and was healed. The women at the tomb, unafraid to face reality, yet joyously surprised, becoming the first evangelists of the resurrection. In Luke 8:1–3 and Mark 15:40–41 we hear of women followers of Jesus. Names of these women disciples appearing in the synoptic gospels include Mary Magdalene, Mary the mother of James and Joseph, Salome, Joanna, and Susanna. In every instance Jesus demonstrated the first-class citizenship of women in the Rule of God and thus in God's world. Do we?

Can we receive the body and blood of Jesus Christ in the eucharist apart from concern for the abuse of women's bodies so widespread in our culture and throughout the world? Spreading the welcome table of Jesus with women is to become an advocate for women's equality and rights across the board. The embodied reality of the eucharist reminds us as Christians to take specific steps toward discouraging violence against women (and everyone else for that matter) at all levels, including abuse within the church, domestic violence, and public violence on the streets and elsewhere.

Carol J. Adams, editor with Marie Fortune of *Violence Against Women and Children: A Christian Theological Sourcebook*, Continuum, 1996, offers much wisdom on sexual abuse. Religious institutions, she says, have responsibility for prevention. Failing that, then intervention. In the absence of those: confession, repentance, and restitution.

The goal of prevention, she reminds us, is to ensure the safety of the vulnerable. Naming the issue encourages the church to avoid being a silent bystander. Naming can be done in preaching, in pastoral conversations, in church school classes, and in the church's newsletter. Everyone is put on notice that sexual abuse is not a taboo subject and that it is unacceptable behavior. Prevention is also served when churches develop written church policies concerning child sexual abuse and battering.

Intervention, Adams says, creates accountability by confronting the abuser. Community structures, such as legal action or therapeutic resources, may be called upon by the church as necessary. These actions offer the hope of a transformative future to both victim and perpetrator. Obviously, these are complex and highly contextualized situations calling for appropriate training and education of both clergy and laity.

If neither prevention nor intervention takes place, the church is called to a very specific confession of failure. Repentance must follow, because repentance involves change in behavior on the part of the church. As a rabbi once said, repentance is when you are faced with the same situation again and you respond in a different manner. Where possible, repentance should be followed by restitution.

The embodied sacrament calls forth Christian concern for the broken bodies among society's most vulnerable members. The eucharist is a sacrament of wholeness out of brokenness.

Spreading the Welcome Table with People of Color

His name was Herb Oiler. He was a non-churchgoing white man with gnarled, arthritic fingers. Barbecue was his specialty. He had a patent on a wood-burning barbecue pit and served the best barbecue in Mesquite, Texas. I met Herb in the early 1960s when I was pastor of St. Stephen Methodist Church. Each week or so I'd cross two highways to drive into old Mesquite, as we called it, to mail the church newsletter. This task could have been delegated, but the truth was, I wanted to visit with Herb.

Herb was a "down-home" man. Nothing fancy, no attempt to impress anyone. Just the best barbecue you can imagine combined with good conversation and common-sense philosophy about life. He would ask about my family and about how the church was doing, even though he wasn't a churchman. Or was he?

You won't be surprised that one day we wandered into a conversation about communion. I'll never forget the observation he shared. He reflected briefly about some members of his wife's congregation when they came to the Oilers' home after taking communion at church. "They barely arrived at our place, with the crumbs of the communion bread still on their clothes when they began to ask, 'What are we going to do about these niggers who are moving into our neighborhood?'" Herb saw and heard this with his own eyes and ears.

He clearly understood the contradiction, even though he wasn't a churchgoer. He just shook his head.

How is it that Christians can worship the God of Jesus Christ and not make connections with what it means to be a good neighbor? I suspect it happens to all of us at least some of the time, maybe in startling ways, maybe more subtly. I can look back on my faith journey and see that in a number of ways unrecognized at the time, the values of the dominant culture simply obscured the connection of worship with ethical attitudes and actions. The unconscious osmosis of cultural values blinded me to the reality of God's freeing grace and the challenge of moral imperatives. Once I recognized the problem, two additional questions immediately surfaced. How might I be blind *now* to other implications of the eucharist and Christian worship? And when I believe I recognize those implications, how do I go about living them amid some of the complexities of our world? Am I willing to take the risks which may be necessary?

Suppose you live in an urban area. Suppose further that the Public Housing Authority is proposing to build some housing units for low-income citizens in your neighborhood. The architecture of the new apartments is to be comparable in appearance with existing single-residence housing and offers an opportunity for low-cost housing to be more evenly distributed in the city rather than centered primarily in one urban sector. The Public Housing Authority has purchased an option on the necessary land.

When this hypothetical scene became reality in North Dallas, the public hearings in preparation were characterized by a storm of protest by the already settled white neighbors: "*These people*—the new incoming neighbors—will not keep up their property. Crime rates will rise. Existing property values will nose-dive. *They* will not be comfortable in our area. *They* will not have sufficient public transportation to get to work, *if* they work."

Some of the area's Christian clergy were interviewed to express their thoughts. One said he hadn't thought about it.

One expressed concern about his parishioners' hard-earned property values. Another said he told his congregation that if this unwanted change took place, they should respond in a civil manner and not obstruct actual construction.

I expect that many of those expressing opposition to the Housing Authority's plan are worshiping Christians on Sunday morning, given the size of churches in the area. The assumptions behind the various objections do not connect with the welcoming hospitality so basic to the eucharist. No welcome table here! The assumptions are all culturally dominated: The incoming neighbors are not "our kind" of people and have nothing but trouble to offer existing residents; the plan will bring an influx of low-income people of color and will thus be a detriment to the neighborhood; they are not as important as our property values; we have no responsibility as citizens to consider the well-being of the whole city; we do not want our children to experience diversity of color, class, or culture; we have nothing to offer them; we know what's best for them.

Is this the best Christians can do? None of these assumptions stand up to a true understanding of the eucharist. The Christ of the welcome table reverses all of the above assumptions. Christ welcomes *all* neighbors to the table, both in and beyond the congregation's worship. In Christ there are no outcasts, no neighborhood borders, no leftover people, no dividing walls. Can we as Christians spread the welcome table?

Spreading the Welcome Table with Gays and Lesbians

A friend of mine, Gerald Hastings, sent me a letter describing the devastating effects of a spring tornado that touched down in the West Texas Community of Saragosa, Texas. The greatest loss of life and injury was centered at the Community Center where the local Head Start program was conducting a "graduation" night program for the families of children transitioning to kindergarten.

At that time my friend was on the staff of Head Start's regional office in Dallas. Gloom and sadness settled over the staff. Eventually it was learned that not one of their enrolled children was killed, although several lost siblings and parents. The letter then offered the following account:

> In the days that followed offers of assistance poured in from all over the country. I was especially impressed with the response of the churches. Baptists offered engineering and architectural help in designing and constructing a new community center. Mennonites, Catholic Men, Adventists, United Methodist Committee on Relief, and many others got together in a coordinated effort to help survivors put their lives and community back together.
>
> ...The following Sunday was communion Sunday at the church where Drue and I worshiped. We always sat in a balcony pew as if we had a long-term lease on it. Balcony worshipers were always served last. I was still hurting from the Saragosa experience as I watched the congregants move toward the altar, kneel, and receive the elements. There we were, older and younger, wealthy and welfare recipients, a mix of race and ethnicity, a large contingent of gays and lesbians. In a congregation that was not free of bias and quite capable of being mean-spirited towards people a bit different, we were kneeling uncomfortably close to one another, drawn by a broken body and spilt blood. Just like Saragosa.
>
> That experience did not explain to me why the violence of nature left some of our children orphans. But it did and still does remind me that brokenness and blood draws believers together in spite of any other differences. (Hastings 1997)

I'm always grateful upon hearing stories of the church at its best. People working together to restore the future for others in great pain. The Lord's Table welcoming all, calling forth wholeness in brokenness, healing in the midst of devastation. When the church is the church, we don't need to debate its relevance. When the church is a haven for people treated as outcasts, instead of an instrument of exclusion, there is cause for joy and gratitude.

Yes, brokenness and spilt blood draws us together in spite of all differences, whether at the welcome table in Christian worship or in the aftermath of a spring tornado in a small town. Suffering reveals our common humanity and dispels stereotypes which place people in boxes convenient to our own prejudices. Did the man robbed and beaten on the road to Jericho quibble over being cared for by a Samaritan?

Have those of us who are heterosexual listened to the stories of gays and lesbians as they recount their experiences with the church and with their families who claim to be Christians? There are certainly exceptions, but far too many experiences negate Christian love and justice: Cast out by the family and virtually disowned, perceived as an abomination, the worst sinners of all, presumed to be pedophiles and not to be trusted around children, emotionally disturbed, don't ask, don't tell. All of this response by heterosexuals in the name of Jesus Christ?

It is not just the oppression of gays and lesbians by church and society that deserves the attention of the church. Many gays and lesbians are baptized Christians, not strangers among us. They *are* the church already, whether the church recognizes it or not. The church has made promises to welcome and nurture and love. Even beyond the fact of baptism, and most important of all in my mind, is the simple fact that gays and lesbians are *human beings* created by God and thus of sacred worth. The church has no warrant to practice cruelty to anyone nor to reject anyone on the basis of race, nationality, gender, class, or sexual orientation. Our warrant is to welcome, to learn and grow together, to embrace in all our foibles and frailties the great commandment to love God and neighbor.

Imagine a congregation where "straights" and "out of the closet" lesbians and gays worship, study, and witness together; where there are no second-class members; where friendships are formed and people's prejudices melt away; where fear and ignorance no longer hold sway.

What an enlightened journey Fran and I have been privileged to share with Northaven United Methodist Church in
Dallas. I'm not claiming perfection for Northaven, just a community with a growing concept of family. The lesbian and
gay members have found a welcoming community where
they can offer their gifts of prayers, talents, service, and attendance. We all share in a mixed-orientation congregation
that tends to mirror the real world of work and family and
society.

Many of the straight members have made gay and lesbian friends for the first time and have realized that we are
all basically alike, with the exception of sexual orientation.
We hurt and hope alike. The same blood types run through
our veins. We are computer programmers, sales people, staff
members of community agencies, counselors, you name it.
We share the eucharist, sing in the choir, pay our pledges,
serve on committees, show up at work days around the
church, and participate in the mission of the church. We are
part of God's family and thus part of each other.

Few of us will forget the words of Mike Merrifield at his
last Northaven worship service. He had been an active member for some time. We had observed Mike's journey as a person with AIDS from robust health to a cane to a walker to a
wheelchair. During the concerns he thanked the congregation for loving support in times of both good and bad health
and concluded with these words: "This week I found Christ
in my mailbox. I'll always be grateful." Two weeks later Mike
died. I was never so grateful for Northaven and for those
members who had mailed cards and letters of support to
Mike in his final days. This is what I call spreading the welcome table.

Scripturally, we do well to listen to Jesus above all. For
me the clarity of his love by word and deed in scripture carries more weight than a few biblical texts that are flawed by
patriarchal conditioning. Surely we cannot be morally instructed by an archaic text in which daughters are offered
for sexual abuse and God is portrayed as a righteous mass

killer (Genesis 19). Nor do I believe that Paul offers God's final word on matters of gender. After all, Paul instructed Christians that women should not speak in church (1 Corinthians 14:34–35).

There is absolutely no evidence that lesbians and gays are less inclined or less able and willing than heterosexuals to love God and neighbor; no evidence of less ability or inclination for compassion, justice, feeding the hungry, clothing the naked, or welcoming the stranger. What is most important in Jesus' life and message is what needs to be most important for all who bear the name Christian. Are we Christians known by our love? I believe it is way past time for the church to become not only a welcoming community for lesbians and gays but also an advocate for full human, legal, and civil rights.

Spreading the Welcome Table with Persons with Disabilities

There are 43 million people with disabilities in the United States. I didn't know this until I did research for this section. America's largest minority includes people with physical, psychological, and intellectual impairments and their consequent disabilities. Illnesses, accidents, genetic conditions, violence, and aging all contribute to disabling conditions.

I have chosen to use the phrase "persons or people with disabilities" in the belief that it may be the most acceptable and unifying to all concerned. Of course people with disabilities strongly affirm the right to choose their own self-descriptive terms, a right the church should support. Some of the terms used are: persons who are disabled, differently abled, physically challenged, and handicapped. My purpose here is not to examine the various implications, the pros and cons. Suffice it to say there are strong feelings about these descriptions among persons with disabilities. Those of us who are currently able-bodied need awareness of this. It is also my understanding that disability language is unacceptable to many deaf persons, especially those who from birth have been part of deaf culture communicated by American sign language.

A distinction may be made between having a disability and being handicapped. Christine M. Smith states:

> I believe that being handicapped is an experience of oppression that is the direct repercussion of living with a disability in a world that is unwilling to address the needs, gifts, and very existence of people with disabilities…It is an environment of discrimination or oppression that causes a disability to become handicapping. (Smith 1992, 18–19)

An environment of discrimination unfortunately has been and often remains an apt description of the church in relation to people with disabilities. Has the church listened to the stories and experiences of people with disabilities? Have we provided access to our buildings for people using wheelchairs? Do we try to understand how our language is perceived by persons with disabilities? Are people with disabilities considered a threat to our society's ideal of the perfect or desirable body, or a reminder of the contingency of our own able-bodied health or of existence itself?

By and large the church has been sorely remiss in educating our clergy and our congregations in the particularities of spiritual, economic, cultural, and political oppression of people with disabilities. Many of us have been more aware of white racism, sexism, and classism than we are of handicappism. Some of us were deeply involved in civil rights issues years ago (and continue to be), as it pertained to white racism, and more recently in advocacy for women's rights, as well as gay and lesbian rights. Only more recently is the church in some quarters beginning to acknowledge a wake-up call in responding to people with disabilities.

The church should not regard these matters simplistically or naively. We're talking about some fundamental revisioning in our theological reflections and the likelihood of financial expenditures in the midst of an already tight budget. Saint

Paul School of Theology in Kansas City, Missouri, where I served as president for twelve years, was situated on an old campus with many old buildings. The campus had been the home of National College and its predecessor, the National Training School for Methodist deaconesses. No thought had been given to updating these buildings for disability access. As a young seminary we had a small endowment and an underpaid faculty and staff. In fact, in my first couple of years the faculty volunteered with reluctance to take a pay cut in order to avoid a faculty reduction.

Our financial situation slowly improved, but not enough to do what we would have liked to do in the way of salary improvement. In the meantime the matter of accessing our buildings presented itself. I went over the entire campus with a person who used a wheelchair in order to gain a fresh perspective. Many conversations and deliberations with individuals and groups followed. An ethical dilemma loomed before us: use our meager resources for salary enhancement on behalf of an underpaid faculty, some of whom had served the seminary faithfully for a number of years, or spend what was available for ramps, restroom repairs, and other accessing needs?

We managed to raise some funds for campus access on a plan designed for progress in stages over a period of time. We developed a plan and did what we could manage. We became intentional. This experience alerted me to the reality that difficult choices may have to be made. Sometimes saying yes to this means saying no to that. It goes with the administrative territory, and with the life of faith.

Much is at stake for the church as well as for people with disabilities. Valuing persons with disabilities is more than a matter of goodwill or benevolence. Justice and equality are at stake internally and for the church's witness to the larger community. We dismember Christ's body when we fail to be fully welcoming to persons with disabilities. When the Lord's table is not spread to encompass disability, either literally or figuratively, the church loses a source of growth and learning for the currently able-bodied members. The gifts of resourcefulness and persistence offered by persons with disabilities is lost to the church, a treasure greatly needed. Also lost is a source of wisdom and strength often available to temporarily able-bodied persons from persons with disabilities.

What might a theology and practice of spreading the welcome table to persons with disabilities embrace? Here is a ten-point agenda:

- Listening to persons with disabilities, welcoming their stories, and shaping the church's response accordingly

- Affirming the right to name their own choice of terms

- Including persons with disabilities in all discussions and plans to become fully welcoming and inclusive

- Creating an atmosphere of mutuality; that is, making the church aware that it needs the presence of people with disabilities, just as the church is needed by people with disabilities

- Getting in touch with the church's history in relation to people with disabilities, including presuppositions and practices

- Becoming aware of the disability rights movement and legislation regarding disability, especially the Americans with Disabilities Act (ADA) of 1990

- Acknowledging present discrimination, educating church members, and developing an intentional plan to begin the necessary steps to provide access

- Regarding inclusion as a justice issue with a biblical and theological foundation

- Becoming intentional not only in full access to all church buildings and spaces (such as rest rooms) but also access to positions of responsibility and decision making at the most significant levels, including ordained ministry

- Moving toward public awareness through advocacy for the rights and needs of people with disabilities

The eucharist of the wounded, yet victorious Host presents a special coming together of persons with disabilities and persons temporarily able-bodied. In her book *The Disabled God (Toward a Liberation Theology of Disability)*, Nancy L. Eiesland has provided me with deep insights:

> Hope and the possibility of liberation welling up from a broken body is the miracle of the eucharist. At the table, we remember the physical reality of that body for a people broken. At the table, we understand that Christ is present with us. As the disabled God, Christ has brought grace, and in turn, makes us a grace to others as physical beings...(Eiesland 1994, 114–116)

The eucharist as body practice signifies solidarity and reconnection: God among humankind, the temporarily able-bodied with people with disabilities, and we ourselves with our bodies. In the eucharist, we encounter the disabled God, who displayed the signs of disability, not as a demonstration of failure and defect, but in affirmation of connection and strength. In this resurrected Christ, the nonconventional body is recognized as sacrament. Christ's solidarity with the more than 600 million people with disabilities worldwide is revealed in the eucharist.

This understanding of the eucharist, therefore, must reject the image of the "perfect body" as an oppressive myth. In the United States, where a fetish for perfect bodies drives people to self-flagellation in overzealous exercise, to mutilation through plastic surgery, to disablement in eating disorders, and to warehousing and stigmatizing people with disabilities, young and old, the eucharistic message that affirms actually existing bodies is desperately needed and offers healing body practices. This affirmation differs from a romanticization of the body, male or female. Instead it acknowledges the ambiguous character of embodiment and affirms our existence as painstakingly, honestly, and lovingly embodied beings. (Eiesland 1994, 116)

These insights remind us that the church needs to distinguish between cure and healing; that is, one's physical condition is not necessarily descriptive of one's wholeness or lack of it.

Concluding Reflection

This chapter has presented some ways in which the eucharist makes a difference in the lives of Christians and others as we seek to live our faith in today's world. My purpose is not to overwhelm readers with a vast array of imperatives, but to indicate the directions of grace in which the eucharist leads us in the name and example of Jesus Christ. From an expanding awareness of these several directions one might choose one or two for specific personal attention and advocacy, sharing with others similarly concerned. We have it on good authority that Christ himself will come to us at a deep level as we seek to love our neighbors and receive their God-given gifts for us. (See Betenbaugh 1997 in sources cited.)

My path over the years in seeking to live the eucharist in today's world has led from abdication to awareness to accompaniment to advocacy. All this in the desire to respond faithfully to God's calling, yet filled with slowness of learning and not a little resistance on my part, even as I have experienced God-given liberation and joy. Sometimes I name it as movement from "duh" to "oh-oh" to "ahah" to "yes, but." Can you find yourself on this continuum?

7

Liturgies, Logistics, and Language

In the process of liturgical revision, it became apparent
that when choices had to be made they were generally
between late-medieval practices mediated through
Cranmer or early-Christian services documented by
Hippolytus. In almost every case, the preference was
for early Christian over late medieval.
(White, Protestant Worship, 1989, 169)

Liturgies

While this statement by James White pertains to recent
United Methodist liturgical revision, it points in a direction
taken by several church traditions in the post–Vatican II era.
This post–Vatican II emphasis may be briefly summarized
by several liturgical choices and practices.

The liturgies of the early church have reinstituted the
Great Prayer of Thanksgiving as the backbone of the eucharistic liturgy. As noted in chapter 3, this results in a strong
emphasis on God's grace as a gift to sinners. The Great Prayer
of Thanksgiving embraces a much wider orbit of God's action in creation and history than the more limited words of
institution, which center mainly on the upper room origins
of the supper. The Great Thanksgiving, a synthesis of prayer,

hymn of praise, and creed, is a Christian version of the Jewish table blessing. It is sometimes called the prototype of the central prayer of the central act of Christian worship, and it ordinarily relies on a number of scriptural references.

The Great Thanksgiving commonly opens with an introductory dialogue between liturgist and people. A typical example:

> The Lord be with you.
> And also with you.
> Lift up your hearts.
> We lift them up to the Lord.
> Let us give thanks to the Lord.
> It is right to give our thanks and praise.
>   (*UMH* 1989, 9–11) .

The introductory dialogue may be followed by a statement of thanksgiving for God's mighty acts. Reference is frequently made to God's act in creation, a typical emphasis in the Eastern liturgy. Deliverance from captivity, covenant making, and God's speaking through the prophets of Israel testify to God's action in history as perceived through faith.

The sanctus from Isaiah 6:3 and the benedictus from Psalm 118:26/Matthew 21:9 can be said or sung by the people. The Thanksgiving continues with focus on God's action through Jesus Christ. Specific words of thanksgiving will vary according to the Christian year, thus providing a variety of themes.

The eucharistic liturgy may then call forth the words of institution from the Last Supper, lifting up Jesus' words related to bread and cup in remembrance of him. As noted above, these words from the biblical accounts of the upper room constitute the basic liturgy of communion for many congregations. (Examples of eucharistic liturgy in this chapter are from pp. 9–11 of *The United Methodist Hymnal* unless otherwise noted.) However, a review of *The Book of Common Worship* of the Presbyterian Church U.S.A., (1993), *Lutheran Book of Worship* (1978, 6th printing 1985), *The United Methodist Hymnal* (1989), *The United Methodist Book of Worship* (1992),

Book of Worship: United Church of Christ (1986), the Episcopal *Book of Common Prayer* (1979), and *Chalice Worship* (Disciples of Christ, 1997) reveals a widespread use of Prayers of Thanksgiving. To be sure, these include the words of institution but place them in a considerably wider context.

The words of institution may be followed by appropriating Jesus' words into the present (anamnesis). This part of the prayer could sound like this:

> In remembrance of these your mighty acts in Jesus
>   Christ,
> we offer ourselves in praise and thanksgiving
> as a holy and living sacrifice,
> in union with Christ's offering for us...

Some traditions respond with an acclamation:

> Christ has died, Christ is risen, Christ will come again.

Then may follow an invoking of the Holy Spirit through a petition for sanctification of gifts and those who receive them:

> Pour out your Holy Spirit on us gathered here,
>   and on these gifts of bread and wine.
> Make them be for us the body and blood of Christ,
> that we may be for the world the body of Christ,
>   redeemed by his blood.
> By your spirit make us one with Christ,
>   one with each other,
>   and one in ministry to all the world,
> until Christ comes in final victory
>   and we feast at his heavenly banquet.

The Great Prayer of Thanksgiving concludes with a trinitarian doxology, followed by the Lord's Prayer, the breaking of the bread, the lifting of the cup, and the giving or distribution of the elements to the people.

There is a fourfold framework for thanksgiving and communion: taking the bread, giving thanks, breaking the bread (and lifting the cup), and giving the bread and cup. This historic fourfold action is practiced with some variation in the gospel accounts of the Last Supper, in the Emmaus experience of the risen Lord at table, and in the feeding stories of Mark 6 and 8.

The study of denominational books of worship and hymnals reveals both commonality and diversity, as might be expected. Here are just a few very brief snapshots:

1. From the *Presbyterian U.S.A. Book of Common Worship*

The eucharist is appropriately celebrated as often as on each Lord's Day (p. 41). This fits the trend in several denominations for more frequent communion, although the actual practice in many congregations is monthly. I was impressed that one of the optional invitations to the Lord's table is that of joyful feast taken in part from Luke 24. The terms Lord's supper and eucharist are both prominent.

2. From the *Lutheran Book of Worship*

Three settings for holy communion are provided. The Great Thanksgiving is similar in content and order as described earlier in this chapter. The hymnody section reflects the importance of congregational participation in eucharistic music.

3. From *The United Methodist Book of Worship*

There are five services of word and table recommended for use in *The United Methodist Book of Worship*. The first three reflect the choice of early Christian influence over the late-medieval service with its immediate roots via John Wesley and Thomas Cranmer. Service 4 comes from the rituals of the former Methodist and Evangelical United Brethren churches. It resonates with the medieval flavor of penitential piety and recurring focus on sacrifice. Service of Word and Table V is titled "With Persons Who Are Sick or Homebound."

4. From the *United Church of Christ Book of Worship*

There is a move toward word and sacrament being normative, but this is optional. The manner of distribution is not prescribed. The communion prayer may be given in the pastor's own words, although there is recognition of the Great Prayer of Thanksgiving in a similar fashion as described above. Inclusive language is regarded as important. Gender-specific language for God is avoided as a matter of policy.

5. *From the Episcopal Book of Common Prayer*

The Holy Eucharist is referred to as the principal act of Christian worship on the Lord's Day (p. 13). Several eucharistic rites are given with a variety of eucharistic prayers under the heading The Great Thanksgiving. In each prayer Jesus' words of institution, the sanctus, and reference to the Holy Spirit are common elements. The terms Lord's Table and altar are used interchangeably.

6. *From Chalice Worship, Christian Church (Disciples of Christ)*

Chalice Worship provides several models for the Lord's supper. These have been informed by Christian practices in the first four centuries, generally following the pattern set forth by Justin Martyr. A study of "Lord's Day Service I & II" suggests ecumenical influence combined with Disciples heritage: "Two contemporary Disciples models of worship influenced by recent ecumenical studies of early Christian worship are presented here. They express different ways of reflecting Disciples heritage within this common understanding...A third Lord's Day service is also given, which has been designed by the Consultation on Church Union for ecumenical or general use" (*Chalice Worship* 1997, 5). Disciples utilize a strong presence of lay leadership in the service of the Lord's supper.

During my pastorates from 1958–1973 we nearly always used the term Lord's supper or holy communion. The use of the term eucharist has become widespread in the past quarter century in the United Methodist Church, along with the other names. The research resulting from Vatican II (1962–65) and the corresponding seminary training have unleashed liturgical preference for the practices of the early church.

If I were a pastor today, I would encourage the use of these several eucharistic liturgies throughout the year. As my wife claims, we need not recall the whole gamut of salvation history at every eucharistic celebration. Sometimes a liturgy with fewer words and perhaps more focus on the Last Supper story or on the Emmaus meal is desirable. The Great Thanksgiving is a broad liturgical panorama, and we need this, too. In liturgy I believe in employing enough of the familiar to provide stability and continuity while practicing sufficient variation to reveal the many-splendored gifts of our rich liturgical treasury. Each tradition, however, determines its own framework and polity for flexibility in the sacramental rite.

Until now I have avoided much comment on the various names for the sacrament, preferring that we use the various terms more or less interchangeably. Now a brief sketch of the terms might be helpful. (Stookey 1993, 172–74). *Eucharist* is the oldest naming, and it is composed of two ancient Greek roots: *eu,* a prefix meaning "good" or "well" and *charis,* meaning "gift" or "grace." This emphasis on gratitude and thanksgiving is an antidote to the notion of mere recollection of a long-ago crucified Lord. Orthodox, Catholic, and Protestant traditions use the term eucharist.

Mass is the usual Roman Catholic expression for the form of the eucharistic liturgy. *The Lord's supper,* used by Protestant reformers, denotes a meal, and yet seems to limit our understanding of the sacrament to the Last Supper in the upper room without connection to the Emmaus experience.

Holy communion implies a sharing between God and people as well as people with people. Anglicans, Methodists, and Lutherans have used the term to indicate the entire sacramental liturgy, although the term communion can also refer to the act of receiving the elements.

Logistics

Churches that celebrate the eucharist every Lord's Day have known for years that word and table reinforce each other and can be observed within an acceptable time limit without haste. The use of intinction and reliance on serving "stations," that is, several locations in the sanctuary, makes it possible for large congregations to commune weekly without taking time from a twenty-minute sermon. This, of course, applies to the practice of coming forth from the pews or chairs in order to receive the elements.

Traditions that have bishops—Roman Catholic, Episcopalian, United Methodist, and the Evangelical Lutheran Church—observe the eucharist by coming forward. Non-episcopal traditions usually partake of the elements in the pew. I'm not sure what the connection is here, but that's the way it works. Coming forward has a number of connotations: being called out, as God called forth Israel from bondage in Egypt and as Jesus called the disciples to come forth; according to some, a more purposeful way of responding to Jesus as table host or to God's sacrificial action; an opportunity to kneel at the communion railing where this is practiced; an acting out the biblical, theological story of God's people as a pilgrim people on journey.

The advocates of celebrating the eucharist in the pew speak thusly: God comes to us in the form of bread and cup where we are and as we are; the priesthood of all believers is more faithfully enacted as laypersons give and receive from each other; a more communal experience occurs, especially when all receive simultaneously; going forward seems to portray a cafeteria mentality and may appeal to the instinct to be seen by others.

Where it is allowable within liturgical rubrics and guidelines I believe it is worthwhile to vary the process and means by which we receive. Why should it be the same every time? A reasonable variation can reveal new meanings and bring to the surface a greater range of biblical stories for life today.

Over many years I have given the bread and cup in a variety of settings: in the front, in the pews; sitting, standing, and kneeling; bread served in many forms and usually grape juice for most United Methodists, but sometimes wine in other churches; by intinction and from communion trays or from a communal chalice. The form of the bread may vary according to the culture. We all have our preferences, but it is to be hoped they are flexible enough to avoid prejudices. The eucharist is much too rich to be incarcerated within the confines of a narrow mind.

Today more and more congregations in several denominations are moving towards more frequent communion, if not in every service of the Lord's Day, then perhaps at an early service and/or in a midweek service.

Language

The language of the liturgy is firmly established in some traditions. In other church bodies there is more freedom, for better or worse, to make language choices. Ordained clergy in most churches have control over language in parts of the liturgy such as sermons and pastoral prayers. But what about eucharistic liturgy?

Much has been written about the power of language and the power of naming. In recent years, for example, hymnal committees have wrestled with exclusive and inclusive language. If the church is truly to be a welcoming community at the Lord's table, our table language should be as inclusive as possible within the various circumstances in which we worship.

Liturgical language can be inclusive in many ways. Inclusiveness embraces language sensitivity in relation to gender, class, race, age, and disability. Not to be discounted is eucharistic liturgy, which embraces a global awareness and a cultural sensitivity to both people and environment.

Furthermore, as Marjorie Procter-Smith has astutely pointed out in her book *In Her Own Rite*, language in reference to God comes in three forms: the verbal language of prayer, song, acclamation, and creed; the kinesthetic (or physical) language of gesture, posture, and movements; the visual language of art, icon, and space (Procter-Smith 1990, 62). Her chapters 3 and 4 offer much-needed provocative insights into language about humanity and God from the standpoint of constructing a feminist liturgical tradition.

Procter-Smith suggests there are three ways to wrestle with the problem of male-centered liturgical language. These are distinct and yet not necessarily opposing viewpoints. *Nonsexist* language avoids gender-specific terms. It is sex-blind. An example is functional God language of Creator, Redeemer, and Sustainer for the Trinity. The drawback here is "the tendency for hearers to interpret nongender-specific language as male" (Procter-Smith 1990, 64).

Inclusive language includes female references, perhaps balanced with male references. "This approach not only restores color and clarity to language; it also encourages the inclusion of names of women to balance the names of men" (Procter-Smith 1990, 65). Even when balanced in God language, however, the female images are likely to be devalued in our male-dominated family.

Emancipatory language is a challenging and transforming method that transforms degraded terms into words of pride and power, such as *black pride, chicano/chicana,* and *women.* Emancipatory language makes women visible and is "necessary in order to move beyond the limits of androcentric language to the generation of a new vision and a new way of speaking about that vision" (Procter-Smith 1990, 67). "Emancipatory language assumes that God is engaged in women's struggles for emancipation, even to the point of identifying with those who struggle" (Procter-Smith 1990, 66).

The first step in any constructive change is awareness of a discrepancy between what is and what can be and should be. Awareness leads to inquiry and the search for improvements and solutions. For example, what does the liturgy of the eucharist say to worshipers when God is always referred to as male? when the eucharist is always administered by males? when our visual art surrounding the worship experience excludes people of color or portrays women as dependent? Do our gestures and symbols suggest dominance or mutuality? How do ordained ministers utilize the authority for which they are ordained in a way that honors the baptism and ministry of all Christians?

I can retrace part of my own journey in relation to language sensitivity by reviewing my sermons over the years and the books I have published. I'm still learning. What is clear enough is that I became convinced of the power of language to create what it names. In the 1970s I began to strive for inclusive language referring to humans. God was next. Biblical studies reveal female images of God in scripture as well as in church history. Similarly important, I began to hear the pain and sense of exclusion from my sisters resulting from exclusive language. Thus both biblical and pastoral concerns prompted change.

Marjorie Procter-Smith states, "As an aspect of God represented as a woman, Sophia or Wisdom, personified God's creative activity in the world as well as God's companionship with humankind. Sophia gave knowledge of God, salvation, and peace to humanity" (1990, 92–93). The wisdom tradition is most prominent in the Protestant Canon in Proverbs, Job, and Ecclesiastes, as well as in many of the Psalms.

Today biblical scholars are recovering the tradition of female images of God. We see examples in Isaiah 42:14: "I will cry out like a woman in labor, I will gasp and pant." Similar images are to be found in Isaiah 49:14–15, 66:12–13, and Hosea 11:1, 4. Meister Eckhart in the thirteenth century and Julian of Norwich in the fourteenth century both spoke of female images of God.

Language is a difficult issue in liturgy and calls for careful consideration of many issues: the androcentric and patriarchal character of the Bible, as well as much of church tradition; the sense of exclusion felt by many women in response to exclusive language; and the implications of strictly male language for God over a period of time that "there is 'common ground' between God and men which does not exist between God and women" (Procter-Smith 1990, 62).

My personal witness is this: If we believe God's love values all people equally, our language should also value all people equally. No one claims this is a simple task. What I do claim is that we have before us a very important task.

8

If All Else Fails

Come, Come!
Come and celebrate the supper of the Lord.
Let's make an enormous loaf of bread,
Let's bring abundant wine,
Like the wedding at Cana.

Women, don't forget the salt.
Men, bring along the yeast.
Come, guests. Come, many guests!
You who are lame, blind, crippled, poor.

Come quickly!

Let's follow the recipe our Lord gave us.
All of us, let's knead the dough together
*   with our hands.*
See how the bread rises,
Watch the joy.

For today we celebrate a meeting with our Lord.
Today we renew our commitment to the Kingdom.
Nobody should go hungry any more.

(Tamez)

Here is a eucharistic invitation for all seasons. On first glance it might seem to be appropriate only for the Latin American culture from which it arose. In a more symbolic or metaphorical sense, however, the words speak universally.

Come and celebrate. Everyone is a participant in one way or another. The welcome table beckons us all: the lame, the blind, the crippled, the poor. A joyful feast. We meet the Lord. Our commitment is renewed. No one need go hungry any more, spiritually or physically. A true eucharist. A sacrament deeply personal and deeply public.

In the fourteenth century Catherine of Siena, a member of third order Dominican laity, committed herself to witnessing for the unity of the church during a time of schism related to the papacy. She sacrificed her body for the unity of the church during her final months, consuming only the eucharistic Host.

Her sacrifice could well be a metaphor for Christians today, namely, the eucharist is an expression of the fullness of God's revelation, and thus central to the life of the church and to our lives. As we have seen, to participate in the eucharist is to be fed at the deepest level in a way that frees us for the sacred struggle of feeding others with the divine manna of love and justice.

My friend George Baldwin was a member of the Saint Paul School of Theology faculty (United Methodist) in Kansas City during my time of service there in the late 1970s and early 1980s. Over a period of time his faith journey led him to resign from the faculty, to give away virtually all of his material goods, and to commit his life to living among the poor. As he put it, "God has called me to be poor and to live in solidarity with the poor." As a consequence he went to Nicaragua, learned Spanish for the first time at age fifty, and lived for a number of years among the people in both rural and urban areas. Presently, he is working for the poor through various ministries in the United States.

During his college days many years ago he recalls a summer when he assisted his grandfather in Montana in keeping bees. Grandfather, a retired Methodist clergyman, was a spartan individual, living simply and close to nature. On one occasion George asked him, "Grandfather, what's the basic minimum you could live on? What could you get by on?" Grandfather thought a minute and replied, "Bread and wine." And, George adds, "that came from a man who never touched a drop of alcohol."

Bread and wine. The everlasting supper, for all seasons and circumstances. We may come to our wits' end, but we need not come to hope's end. If all else fails, receive the eucharist.

Works and Sources Cited

Arias, Mortimer. 1984. *Announcing the Reign of God*. Philadelphia: Fortress Press.

Balasuriya, Tissa. 1979. *The Eucharist and Human Liberation*. Maryknoll, N.Y.: Orbis Books.

Betenbaugh, Helen. 1997. I am indebted to Helen Betenbaugh for discussion and helpful insights.

Birch, Bruce. 1991. *Let Justice Roll Down*. Louisville: Westminster/Knox Press.

The Book of Common Prayer, According to the Use of the Episcopal Church. 1979. New York: The Church Hymnal Corporation.

Book of Common Worship. 1993. Prepared by the Theology and Worship Unit for the Presbyterian Church USA and the Cumberland Presbyterian Church. Louisville: Westminster/John Knox Press.

Book of Worship: United Church of Christ. 1986. New York: United Church of Christ Office for Church Life and Leadership.

The Book of Worship for Church and Home. 1964. An Order of Worship for Such as Would Enter into or Renew Their Covenant with God (John Wesley). Nashville: The United Methodist Publishing House.

Boff, Leonardo. 1980. *Way of the Cross—Way of Justice*. Maryknoll, N.Y.: Orbis Books. Cited by Robert McAfee Brown, *Spirituality and Liberation*. 1988: p. 91.

Brilioth, Yngve. 1961. *Eucharistic Faith and Practice: Evangelical and Catholic*. London: SPCK.

Bromiley, Geoffrey W. 1985. *Theological Dictionary of the New Testament.* Grand Rapids: Eerdman's Publishing Company.

Brown, Robert McAfee. 1988. *Spirituality and Liberation.* Louisville: The Westminster Press.

Chalice Worship. 1997. Compiled and edited by Colbert S. Cartwright and O.I. Cricket Harrison. St Louis: Chalice Press.

Eiesland, Nancy L. 1994. *The Disabled God.* Nashville: Abingdon Press.

Gray, Elizabeth Dodson. 1994. *Sunday School Manifesto.* Wellesley, Mass: Roundtable Press.

Hastings, Gerald L. 1997. From his letter, used by permission.

Henderson, J. Frank and Kathleen Quinn and Stephen Larson. 1989. *Liturgy, Justice, and the Reign of God.* New York: Paulist Press.

Herzog, Frederick. 1988. *God-Walk.* Maryknoll N.Y.: Orbis.

Jordan-Lake, Joy. 1996. *The Christian Century,* "For You and You," Chicago: October 23.

King, Martin Luther, Jr. 1963. *Strength to Love.* Philadelphia: Fortress Press.

Luther, Martin. 1519. "Treatise on the Blessed Sacrament." Quoted on p. 101, *The Reign of God,* Henderson, Quinn and Larson. New York: Paulist Press, 1989.

Lutheran Book of Worship. 1978. Minneapolis: Augsburg Publishing House.

McClain, William B. 1997. "Worship Arts," *The Fellowship of United Methodists in Music and Worship Arts,* March-April.

McElvaney, William K. 1971. *The Saving Possibility.* Nashville: Abingdon Press.

Paldiel, Mordecai, 1996. *Sheltering the Jews: Stories of Holocaust Rescuers.* Minneapolis: Fortress Press.

Power, David N. 1985. *Worship,* Vol. 59, Number 5, September, "Forum: Worship After the Holocaust," pp. 447-455.

Procter-Smith, Marjorie. 1990. *In Her Own Rite.* Nashville: Abingdon Press.

Richardson, Cyril C., ed. 1953. *Early Christian Fathers,* "First Apology of Justin." Philadelphia: The Westminster Press.

Robertson, Robert L. 1997. Taken from his July 25, 1997, article about Josephine United Methodist Church, *United Methodist Reporter.*

Robinson, Sister M. 1985. Quoted by John Koenig. *New Testament and Hospitality.* Philadelphia: Fortress Press. Also quoted on p. 104. *Liturgy, Justice, and The Reign of God.*

Smith, Christine. 1992. *Preaching as Weeping, Confession and Resistance.* Louisville: Westminster/John Knox.

Sobrino, Jon, S.J. 1989. Words spoken by Sobrino, colleague of the six Jesuits murdered November 16, 1989 at an Interfaith Prayer Service, San Francisco, December 1, 1989; reported in *Sojourners,* February-March 1990, p. 6.

Stoesz, John. 1997. I am indebted to John Stoesz of the Greater Dallas Community of Churches for providing information.

Stookey, Laurence Hull. 1993. *Eucharist: God's Feast With the Church.* Nashville: Abingdon Press.

Tamez, Elsa. 1984. "Come and Celebrate The Supper of the Lord," in Cancionero Abierto, Confessing Our Faith Around the World, Faith and Order Paper #123 (III). Geneva:WCC, 1984, America Biblical Seminary. This poem, which is already used widely in various churches, especially for the celebration of the Eucharist, was set to music by Pablo Sosa from Argentina.

Toohey, William. 1984. *Life After Birth: Spirituality for College Students.* New York: Harper.

The United Methodist Book of Worship. 1992. Nashville: The United Methodist Publishing House.

The United Methodist Hymnal. 1989. Nashville: The United Methodist Publishing House.

Voices United. Series for Trial Use. The United Church of Canada. 1996-97.

Watkins, Keith. 1995. *The Great Thanksgiving*. St. Louis: Chalice Press.

Wesley, John. 1944. *Forty-Four Sermons*. London: The Epworth Press.

West, Cornell. 1993. *Race Matters*. Boston: Beacon Press.

White, James F. 1989. *Protestant Worship*. Louisville: Westminster/John Knox Press.

_____. 1990. *Introduction to Christian Worship*. Nashville: Abingdon Press.

_____. 1983. *Sacraments as God's Self-Giving*. Nashville: Abingdon Press.

Yeats, William Butler, 1958. "The Magi," in The Collected Poems of W. B. Yeats. London: MacMillan.